OPEN
WINDOWS IN
BABYLON

OPEN WINDOWS IN BABYLON

The Power of Prayer in a Broken World

KEMELA OKARA

DESTINY IMAGE™ EUROPE srl
Via Maiella, 1
66020 San Giovanni Teatino (Ch) – Italy

"Changing the world, one book at a time."

This book and all other Destiny Image™ Europe books are available at Christian bookstores and distributors worldwide.

To order products, or for any other correspondence:

DESTINY IMAGE™ EUROPE srl
Via della Scafa 29/14
65013 Città Sant'Angelo (Pe) – Italy
Tel. +39 085 4716623 • +39 085 8670146
Email: info@eurodestinyimage.com

Or reach us on the Internet: www.eurodestinyimage.com

ISBN 13: 978-88-96727-32-4
ISBN 13 Ebook: 978-88-96727-36-2
For Worldwide Distribution, Printed in the U.S.A.
1 2 3 4 5 6 / 14 13 12 11

Dedication

This book is dedicated to the memory of my parents, the Honorable Justice (Chief) Robert Okara and Mrs. Esther Okara, who, by example and much love, shaped my life and embedded my values. To them I am eternally indebted.

Acknowledgments

I would like to acknowledge the invaluable support my wife has given me. This book has come at some price. Too often I was too busy to be the loving husband or doting father I should have been.

I also want to say a big thank you to Pastor Tony Rapu for his years of teaching and the example he sets through his lifestyle for many of us to follow.

I thank also all those who at some time or another passed through the School of Spiritual Strategies and the discipleship training at This Present House, Lagos, Nigeria.

Contents

Foreword

Sincerely speaking, when I first took the manuscript of this piece, the first thought that came to my mind was, "Why write another book about prayer?" But I did not need to go far in the book to understand why. This is not just another book on prayer. It's a book by a 21st century person, a greeting to the 21st century people. The challenges that we face today are quite different from the writers of the 19th and 20th centuries.

The challenges of traffic, busy schedules, the Internet, et cetera—all these are a few of the distractions that we all have to cope with today and in the near future. According to global urban studies, most people will be living in cities in the future with distractions, busy schedules, traffic, and technological distractions.

The question now arises, with all these modern urban challenges, how do we find time to pray? What place does prayer occupy in the life of a modern person? How do we combine prayer and spirituality with all the different questions we need to resolve on a daily basis? Pastor Kemela has produced a marvelous work that answers most of the questions of the 21st century person. This book will be especially helpful for professionals and modern normal women who might be tempted to move prayer to a lower place of importance. The insight that Pastor Kemela brings out in this book is refreshing and encouraging. I would like to recommend this book to all the people who want to find a balance between their spiritual life and their professional engagement. Thank you so much, Pastor Kemela, for a brilliant work with so many personal, practical illustrations.

Pastor Sunday Adelaja

Introduction

My motivation in writing this book is quite simple. About 18 years ago, I decided to give Christianity a real try. My parents were devout Anglicans and so we attended church regularly whether we liked it or not. I knew the hymns and the rituals of the church. I knew most of the families who worshiped at the church. I had been baptized and confirmed and could take Holy Communion piously.

But I really didn't have a personal relationship with God. I shied away from a close relationship because I felt the demands of Christianity were impossible. A friend of mine had led me to Christ one quiet Friday evening in January 1992, and so I determined to give Christianity a real try.

Thereafter, I discovered a Pentecostal church meeting in a cinema somewhere in Apapa (a suburb in Lagos, Nigeria, where I lived). I was enthralled at the meeting. The joy, the peace, the warmth, and the worship were all so infectious. At some point, an invitation was made to all who wanted to learn how to pray. I responded enthusiastically to this invitation. Why I did at the time I can't remember, but I suspect it was because I wanted to explore every possible avenue to soak up this new exhilarating experience. Prior to this time my perception of prayer was the perfunctory daily activity of kneeling by my bedside and reciting the Lord's Prayer for a few minutes before getting into bed and dozing off at night.

Since that momentous call, my life has never been the same. It has changed immeasurably. First I discovered that prayer was a lively and vigorous expression focused on God. I learned that not only was it vigorous, it was meant to be full of passion. I learned that public expressions of prayer were meant to be completely uninhibited in speech, posture, and fervency. In other words, it was so different from what I knew to be prayer. So I discovered many more expressions of prayer such as the power of speaking in tongues for extended periods of time. These lessons were eye openers; and since then, my life has never been the same.

Since those spiritual beginnings in the early 1990s I have also gone on to play many different roles in leadership in various local assemblies all around the world—Nigeria, Denmark, and the United Kingdom. Looking back, I now understand that responding to that call to pray was not an accident but something ordained by God to help me discover His will and pursue it—not only that, but to strengthen me and help me withstand the corrupting influence of sin.

JOYS OF PRAYER

Prayer has since become an abiding feature of my life, and so I thought to write about this experience in the hope that it would inspire others as it inspired me to discover the limitless power and possibilities available to us in the joys of prayer. I have preached and taught on prayer over the years such that some people have come to identify me as a prayer warrior, a perception that I am not comfortable with because I don't think God wants to create a special class of people distinguished by their passion to pray.

If anything, just as Moses said to those who found Medad and Eldad prophesying in the camp "I wish that all God's children were prophets" (see Num. 11:29). So also do I wish that every believer irrespective of nationality would be part of the great and joyous family of the Lord fully expressive in the variety of prayer.

PRAYERLESSNESS

Chronic prayerlessness is one of the best-kept secrets I have discovered. To describe it graphically, I would call it spiritual anorexia. I meet men and women who know they ought to cultivate a lifestyle of regular and consistent prayer but seem quite incapable of it! I used to think the reason could be found in our environment or our circumstances. In other words, the challenge of living and working in big cities and the attendant challenges of long hours commuting to and from work, not to talk of the long hours spent at work, which make it impossible, or so it seemed, to cultivate a meaningful prayer time.

For the most part, the challenge, I think, is a lack of revelation or understanding of the critical life and death consequence of prayerlessness. Many do not understand that for the believer—just as oxygen is necessary to stay alive—so is prayer critical to staying alive spiritually. This lack of understanding results in only a few transformed and powerful believers bringing salvation, healing, discipleship and influence to their homes, workplace, community, and nation.

Without a doubt, big cities present some very unique challenges especially where infrastructure is limited. In Lagos, Nigeria, where I live, everyone is familiar with the early morning mad scramble to beat the ubiquitous Lagos traffic. This early morning scramble has grave consequences for our spiritual well-being. Is this unique to Lagos? Not by a long shot. In London where I have also lived, the challenge is the same. Big, congested cities and long commuting distances can pose a special challenge to spiritual vitality.

In the past three years, I have been the resident pastor at This Present House in Lekki, Lagos. Our church is somewhat unique because we have been able to reach the typical professional class found in middle and senior management in many corporate institutions. Also attending are those in the recent wave of Nigerians in the Diaspora returning home; the returnees or "repats" as some would call them. We also have an inner city mission reaching the lower strata of our society such as prostitutes, gang members, drug addicts, etc.

On a regular Sunday at our worship center, called the Dome, we have approximately 2,000 predominantly professional people meeting to worship. A good number of them experience the challenge of cultivating a lifestyle of prayer in the midst of all the demands on their time. As we have worked together teaching, discipling, and fellowshipping, many of the challenges I observed have formed the primary motivation for me to write this book. From our collective experience of the rat race, I realized that many of us are dying slow, spiritual deaths because our circumstances have stifled our spiritual vitality.

THE POWER OF PRAYER

Added to this challenge is the fact that what is now popularly considered "prayer" is devoid of relationship with God. It is more akin to invoking the powers of a God who must be sufficiently induced to exercise His greater power to overcome all our enemies. While of course God wants us to avail ourselves of His power to subdue the works of darkness, the journey to power commences with relationship, union, covenant, and revelation.

We now run the twin risk in this generation of not only losing the dynamic heritage of our fathers in the faith like Watchman Nee, Kenneth Hagin, and many others, we also run the risk of leaving behind a legacy of a reincarnation of the tokens of idol worship in the guise of Christianity. My prayer is that when you finish this book, you will have revelation and an unquenchable desire to be transformed by the power of prayer.

I have, however, witnessed the transformative power of a true understanding of prayer among many with whom I have worked. I therefore feel compelled to write in the hope that our experience would be of immense spiritual benefit to others worldwide. The greatest transformation we all need is to be like Jesus. Since Jesus is the Firstborn among many brethren, we must take advantage of every tool God provides us to be transformed into His image and likeness. I am passionate about believers everywhere being restored to the original plan God had in mind when He made Adam in His image—to have dominion over the earth. We risk talking so much about dominion and not experiencing real dominion that it has become a cliché rather than something we have experienced. So my prayer is that this book will act as a catalyst in bringing about the transformation that God desires to see in all of us. For all those who desire a dynamic prayer life but struggle to attain it, you will find in the following pages insight and practical guidelines to achieve a fruitful and dynamic lifestyle of prayer.

In addition, prayer is also the gateway to the transformative power of God in other areas. It brings about a holistic and revolutionary change to circumstances and situations. I have witnessed the power of prayer to positively transform communities, businesses, ministries, governments, and even nations. Recently I was meditating in the presence of the Lord, and I heard Him clearly say to me that *many times I am limited in what I want to do because there are not enough people praying for My will to come to pass*. It is my prayer that this book will help you see the bigger picture of the power of prayer to go beyond our needs and provide God an opportunity to transform our world through our praying. We must change our current disposition of giving God too little with which to manifest His power and glory in the earth.

There is also the unlimited potential waiting to be unleashed in the life of a praying man or woman and the power that is awakened in the life of a praying man or woman. From my experience, I know that many times I am operating at probably less than 10 percent of my true capacity in Christ. This, I believe, is true of many others too. I have often wondered whether I am exhausting the potential of God for my life for the simple reason that if the Bible says I have been made in the image and likeness of God and that I have the mind of Christ, then I ought to pause and ask myself whether this statement is reflected in my experience. If it is not, then I need to do whatever it takes to make it a reality.

New Dimensions of Life

I have found that prayer as described in this book can unlock a dimension of life and introduce us to an experience of God that we had never imagined possible. For instance, the first time I heard someone talk of praying for hours it seemed impossible and made me think the person was ascetic. But when I also prayed for hours and saw the change that took place in me, I was amazed and then realized that there are dimensions of the life of God waiting to be experienced by the man or woman who breaks the boundaries of society or their circumstances.

It is also my prayer that this book will communicate the unbelievable joys, peace, and alignment with God's ordained destiny that prayer produces in the life of anyone committed to pray. My fervent desire and prayer is that you would unlock something within your "inner man" that connects with the Spirit of God and ushers you into an unbelievable lifestyle. *Prayer is the bridge that connects the natural with the supernatural.* As a result of this truth, I have sought to lay down some principles of the underlying importance of prayer. These signposts introduce a dimension of life that makes dominion, power, rulership, transformation, joy, and peace our daily experience. My fervent desire is that you will experience a revolution in prayer as you read this book.

Transformation and Revolution

Finally, my prayer is that if this book transforms your life and causes a revolution to take place in your prayer lifestyle—that you would seek out others and motivate them to discover what has changed you. We must all be fruitful and multiply the grace and power that God makes available to us. God's desire is that fruitfulness and multiplication are taking place all the time. In your home, your church, your community, go forth and disciple all the men and women you come across in discovering the joys of prayer.

Prayer is the greatest gift we have from God. What other gift can be greater than the gift that transports us into the presence of God? What other gift can be greater than the one that assures us of the voice of God breaking into our world? What other gift can be greater than the one that brings direction and instruction?

Chapter 1

What's the Big Deal About Prayer?

It seems God is limited by our prayer life—that He will do nothing for humanity unless someone asks Him.

—John Wesley

Pray without ceasing (1 Thessalonians 5:17).

Praying always with all [kinds of] prayer and supplication in the Spirit, being watchful to this end with all perseverance and supplication for all the saints (Ephesians 6:18).

One fact we cannot run away from is that prayer is fundamental to staying spiritually alive. It also requires discipline to be consistent. Prayer is like oxygen to our spirit. When we don't pray, it is only a matter of time before we die spiritually.

When counseling others, many times I have found that a majority of the challenges we grapple with are because we are weak—and in many cases, dead spiritually from lack of prayer. This is why Paul exhorted the Christians in Thessalonica to pray without ceasing! We must never forget that as Christians we are an army of occupation regardless of where we are in the world. The whole world lies under the influence of the devil. Every sector of human endeavor is under the influence of the devil. The world environment is deliberately configured to make prayer difficult as a way of life.

To live victoriously and to be tools in the hands of God to advance the agenda of His Kingdom, we need the oxygen of prayer. Imagine if everyone in the worldwide church of Jesus Christ understood this fact. Every believer would become a lethal weapon in the hands of God to overcome the works of darkness in their sphere of influence.

Consistent Prayer

To stay consistent in prayer, it must become a habit. This requires discipline. Our desire to pray will first translate to discipline before we experience the delight of prayer. I have been a Christian now for 18 years. No big deal in itself. Nevertheless, I mention this fact because in the last 18 years I have experienced tremendous grace, favor, and the blessing of God because I developed a desire to pray; and with discipline, I have now discovered the delight of praying consistently.

After 15 years of being a pastor, I have discovered that over 90 percent of the people in the church do not pray consistently. This was a shocking discovery for me. You may wonder how I arrived at this discovery? It came through research during church meetings, discipleship programs, and interaction with believers from different parts of the world over a 15-year period. The million-dollar question I have sought to understand: If prayer is so beneficial, why don't we pray as often as we should?

The simple answer is that prayer is one of the least understood disciplines of Christianity. I meet many pastors who think prayer is simply an avenue for reassuring believers about the goodness of God. I meet others who think prayer is about bringing our wish list to God. Consequently, many believers are hung up on the prayer of the pastor rather than discovering the joys of prayer for themselves. This can be very frustrating, especially when you want to teach the joys of discovering the delights and limitless power of personal access to God. It seems the devil makes a concerted effort to blind us to the real power of prayer. However, we must make a concerted effort to discover why Paul was so emphatic in urging us to *pray without ceasing.*

PRAYER—THE GATEWAY TO GOD'S PRE-ORDAINED PURPOSE

Many things I have learned about prayer in my journey of life are not reflected in books. This has been a very humbling discovery. For a long while I was puzzled at this. There is a deeper significance to prayer that we must all discover. Prayer is fundamentally our gateway to discover what God has pre-ordained even before the heavens and earth were created. After these many years of experiencing some of the joys of prayer, this fact is still mind-boggling to me—even though I have many times experienced the power of prayer in aligning me to God's will.

Prayer is the single most important activity we undertake after we are reconciled to God. It is the pathway to relationship. It is the gateway to power and the assurance of divine revelation in all circumstances. It allows us to breathe in the life of the Holy Spirit, especially when we pray in tongues. It brings a spring to our step as we engage the issues of life on a day-to-day basis. Prayer guarantees us boldness in speech and makes our minds nimble and better able to deal with complex issues of life. It keeps our temperament aligned to that of the Holy Spirit. It releases in us the compassion of God toward others. It releases faith to do the impossible. It enables us to be conversant with the Spirit realm.

All this in turn enables us to be sensitive to the workings of the gifts of the Spirit in us. Prayer diffuses many conflicts before they emerge. It acts as God's gateway of intercession for those in need of salvation, deliverance, rescue, healing, and the grace of God. There is nothing we can do without prayer. This was why Jesus said, "men ought always to pray and not lose heart" (Luke 18:1). Prayer is the activity most feared by the enemy because when we pray, our prayer has the power to dismantle demonic strongholds and all sorts of positive changes begin to happen. Prayer is the catalyst for all divine action. Prayer has the power to cleanse the atmosphere and usher in a peaceable and godly atmosphere. Prayer overcomes sin and temptation because it strengthens our spirit against the onslaught of the devil. Prayer is indispensable.

This is not to say that you and I will not experience our fair share of the ups and downs of life. We will; but prayer will keep us insulated from the negative consequences so that, like Paul, we will say:

> *We are hard-pressed on every side, yet not crushed; we are perplexed, but not in despair; persecuted, but not forsaken; struck down, but not destroyed* (2 Corinthians 4:8-9).

Personally I have known what it is to be pressed on all sides by problems that I thought would crush me under the weight. I can look back today and recognize that prayer insulated me from the crushing power of my problems. I remember a time when we started a business, which soon collapsed under a weight of debt. On every side were creditors and bailiffs looking to secure their interests or the interests of their clients. I was hard pressed indeed. One day I went on a retreat to pray, and God spoke clearly to me from Philippians 3:13-14:

> *…forgetting those things which are behind and reaching forward to those things which are ahead, I press toward the goal for the prize of the upward call of God in Christ Jesus.*

When I received this word, it brought great joy to my soul. Not that my problems instantaneously disappeared, but I knew I wasn't to wallow in the problems but to press forward into my future. This revelation caused me to embrace the future and begin taking steps of faith to discover what lay ahead for me. Consequently, the earlier words of Paul suddenly had a new meaning and a personal resonance. I had been hard-pressed on all sides but yet not crushed. What comfort, what joy!

In the same way, I have faced some very perplexing circumstances such as when my son, who was 5 years old at the time, had a stroke while my wife and I were in South Africa celebrating 10 years of marriage. It was the most baffling turn of events I had ever faced. The state of our minds could only best be imagined. Sometimes even now it still seems unreal. But as we turned to God in prayer, we were soon insulated from the great despair that sought to envelope our hearts.

Rest assured that different kinds of challenges are the lot of life; nevertheless, there is always a way of escape. I am reminded of the words, "Many are the afflictions of the righteous, but the Lord delivers us from them all" (Ps. 34:19). So prayer insulates us from the harsh circumstances of adversity and helps us surf the waves of trials and afflictions as we navigate our way purposefully into the will of God.

A DISCIPLINED APPROACH

The challenge, though, is that for prayer to really be fruitful it requires a disciplined approach. I have struggled with using the word *discipline* because I know some may find it difficult accepting a disciplined approach to something that is intended to bring great joy and great benefit. Others may wonder, considering the difficulty they may have experienced in the past in sustaining a disciplined approach to prayer, whether sustained and disciplined prayer is ever attainable. But the truth is prayer, like every aspect of purposeful living, requires discipline.

Without a doubt, discipline is the key. Our approach to prayer must be very disciplined. From my experience, lack of discipline is one of the most prevalent reasons why people under achieve especially in developing the necessary spiritual lifestyle. Without discipline we cannot have the foundation of prayer. Discipline is as nonnegotiable to praying as breathing is as nonnegotiable to living. Without discipline we will never achieve anything God lays in our hearts to do. It is at the root of most problems.

It was a lack of discipline that led to David's adultery with Bathsheba and ultimately to the murder of Uriah. If David had been disciplined enough to be at the battlefield, he would never have been exposed to seeing Bathsheba bathing. We cannot run away from the necessity of discipline. Unfortunately, an erroneous understanding of grace has filtered into the Body of Christ to the effect that the grace of God is available to make up for areas in our lives where we are not inclined to subject our-selves to any discipline. However, true grace is when I discipline myself to do is what required of me and the enabling grace of God ensures that I am able to then do what I set out in my heart to accomplish.

We must see prayer as the one nonnegotiable fact of spiritual life. This is why, in Paul's exhortation to the believers in Thessalonica captured in the First and Second epistles to the Thessalonians, Paul charged them to *pray without ceasing.* It wasn't that they were to pray without any breaks in between. That would be nonsensical. What Paul meant was that prayer was to be the preeminent activity of their lives. In that Scripture (1 Thess. 5:17), Paul gave the Thessalonians a seven-point charge:

1. To rejoice always;

2. To pray without ceasing;

3. Not to despise prophecies;

4. Not to quench the Spirit;

5. To test all things;

6. To hold fast unto what is good;

7. To avoid all kinds of evil.

Each charge Paul made stands out like a distinct pillar for building our lives into a mighty edifice in God. When it came to prayer, Paul did not suggest that we pray every once in a while. Paul's charge was that we should pray without ceasing. The Amplified Bible puts it this way, "Be unceasing in prayer [praying perseveringly]." While the New International Version describes it as *"pray continually,"* Paul's charge to the Thessalonians was not a suggestion. It was a command. In other words, when I am not engaged in unceasing prayer, I am falling short of God's expectation for me.

WHY PRAY?

The questions are: Why is it so important to God that I pray? Why does He command that my prayer be unceasing? Sometimes it seems as though God demands the impossible! I have discovered, though, that whatever God commands is not impossible. I need to respond in faith. When I do, I discover His grace transports me on eagle's wings. So prayer must be unceasing; men and women everywhere filling up the atmosphere daily with sustained unceasing prayer unto God. My prayer is that you will receive revelation about the unceasing nature of prayer.

When I realized that I needed to pray without ceasing, I made adjustments to my lifestyle. I cut out many activities that were unfruitful. I used to be a television addict. I would spend four to five hours sitting in front of the television screen flicking from one channel to other. After I had been praying for some time, I reflected on all the time I had wasted on television. I realized I had wasted so much precious time investing in meaningless television programs instead of time with God. I have come to realize that many recreational activities are designed to make us dead spiritually and dull intellectually. I was filled with sadness at the realization that I could never recover the time I had ignorantly wasted. So many people are wasting away as they sit in front of their television screens transfixed by the make-believe world in front of them.

For others it is the Internet. Many people are on the Internet for hours not to educate themselves or become part of the wealth-creating opportunities it provides. Rather, they surf all manner of pornographic websites. They can spend hours glued to lewd images that defile the soul and the spirit. They are completely ignorant of the wiles of the devil. The tragedy is that one of the effects of this lifestyle is spiritual anorexia and impotence—a lack of desire for anything spiritual and the inability to overcome it. Unceasing prayer is the only answer for a devil that is unrelenting in his pursuit of every foe. There is much to learn from the examples of Scripture. Israel in the wilderness is illustrative and is aptly described by the psalmist in Psalm 106:13-15 with the words, "They soon forgot His works; they did not wait for His counsel, but lusted exceedingly in the wilderness, and tested God in the desert. And He gave them their request, but sent leanness into their soul." In the same way, we soon forget the works of God, when we do not prayerfully wait for His counsel and instead succumb to the distractions of daily life. This ultimately leads to leanness in our soul.

I know many people who feel they are gainfully occupied at work and therefore find it impossible to maintain unceasing prayer. I deal extensively with this matter in Chapter 2. However, a quick word here. If you are too busy to maintain constant, unceasing relationship with your Creator, then you are out of sync with Him and His world.

A Gateway to Heaven

On one occasion, some disciples prayed in this manner when they heard King Herod had arrested Peter. They knew Peter's life was in grave danger—Herod had already beheaded James the apostle. When Herod saw that it pleased the Jews, he seized Peter also and sought to behead Peter. The believers needed no convincing as to what action to take. They swung into action and "constant prayer was offered to God for him by the church" (Acts 12:5). As they offered unceasing prayer, an angel went into action and supernaturally released Peter. Their prayer was so successful that they didn't believe it when Peter arrived at their door!

To pray without ceasing therefore is to establish a gateway between Heaven and earth. This ensures that every resource from Heaven is constantly flowing into the earth. This is the kind of power that God desires we experience—power that releases angelic activity on earth and power that physically dismantles gates of wickedness and ushers in freedom and liberty to the saints of God.

Who knows what circumstances we overlooked because we did not swing into action like the church did to supernaturally release Peter from the clutches of Herod. This story is very instructive. We notice that the disciples are recorded as offering unceasing prayer. They didn't pray for a while and go home. They were determined to continue until the atmosphere was filled with their words and something had to happen on earth reflecting that change was coming in response to their prayer. Imagine if every married couple understood this principle. Imagine if men and women everywhere caught a revelation of the power of this position. Imagine the earth full of angelic activity dealing with the powers of darkness that underpin different kinds of demonic activity on earth. There is no doubt that in the 21st century the types of demonic activity filtering into marriages, the lives of children, politics and government is greater and subtler than previous generations faced.

Watchman Nee, a great Chinese teacher and author who died under communist rule in China in 1972 for his faith, has this to say on prayer in a collection of his writings titled "The Finest of the Wheat":

> There was once a Christian who well knew how to pray. He declared this, that all spiritual works include four steps: The first step is that God conceives a thought, which is His will: The second step is that God reveals this will to His children through the Holy Spirit, causing them to know that He has a will, a plan, a demand and expectation: The third step is that God's children return His will to Him by praying to Him, for prayer is responding to God's will—if our heart is wholly one with His heart, we will naturally voice in our prayer what He intends to do: And the fourth step is that God will accomplish this very thing....

In other words, what is the use of life if we cannot discern the will of God? Life would be a meaningless grope in the dark. *Prayer, therefore, is the guaranteed access at all times to the will of God.*

Now I must add that there are certain conditions to fulfill all the time. There is, nevertheless, protocol to approaching God. He is the sovereign Lord over all of creation and there are rules about approaching Him, calling upon His name, and representing Him. The psalmist declares in Psalm 24:3-6:

> *Who may ascend into the hill of the Lord? Or who may stand*
> *in His holy place? He who has clean hands and a pure heart,*

who has not lifted up his soul to an idol, nor sworn deceitfully. He shall receive blessing from the Lord, and righteousness from the God of his salvation. This is Jacob, the generation of those who seek Him, who seek your face.

Once our protocol is right, we are guaranteed access to the will of God. Let me illustrate with a principle of law. I trained as a lawyer under the English system of law known as the Common Law. This system of law was later complemented by rules known as the principles of equity. The idea behind the principles of equity was that it would cushion the rigid Common Law rules, which sometimes worked injustice against a party deserving of justice in a court action. However, to benefit from the rules of equity, there was a precondition, which was that, "He who comes to equity must come with clean hands." In other words, to benefit from prayer we must have right standing with God.

When our protocol is right, we can stand before God without condemnation or fear to bring His will to pass on earth. We are the bridge between two realms of existence. We become the conduit through which His will is manifest in the earth. To think that God limits His ability to do anything on earth to the prayer I offer is awe-inspiring. So constant unceasing prayer *is* possible. If God demands it, then it is possible. We must be ready to confront every obstacle in our way to make this our reality. To achieve this we must embrace discipline as a welcome ingredient in our lives.

PUT LIFE INTO PERSPECTIVE

Now discipline is not impossible to achieve when we put life into perspective. This is the first task especially for believers who have gotten used to a wrong theology that wants to supplant a false understanding of grace for discipline. Properly understood, grace and discipline are close companions and coexist side by side comfortably. One helpful definition of grace is God's enablement to do what we ought to do but find difficult to do.

For instance, Paul said of himself, "I labored more than they all, but it was the grace of God at work in me" (1 Cor. 15:10). This is a good illustration of grace. Paul's labor was the product of the grace of God. So grace is not God covering up for my laziness or doing something despite my inaction. It is God supplying the supernatural to complement my efforts. Therefore every step I take as an expression of discipline becomes invaluable material in the hands of God to bring change. When I wake up an hour earlier than usual, grace sees me through the day, even though I may be tired. When I stand in the place of unceasing prayer, grace comes as the strength of God such that now I am doing what I thought was impossible.

It is therefore possible for everyone to experience the power of prayer. It was never God's intention for prayer to be the exclusive preserve of a few. God's desire is that all people create a gateway between Heaven and earth in their families, communities, and nations. Unfortunately for lack of understanding, prayer has more or less come to be seen as the exclusive preserve of a few. We must be a generation of believers who demystify prayer and reintroduce it as a way of life for ourselves and for succeeding generations.

If you don't already have a disciplined approach to prayer, start today! Do not procrastinate. Begin the process of reordering your life. You may need to cancel a subscription to satellite television. You may need to avoid the Internet if you cannot stay away from pornography. Remember, Jesus said if your hand causes you to sin, cut it off. Therefore cut off every opportunity the devil uses to steal your time, defraud your soul, and debauch your spirit. When you do so, you will be amazed at the cleansing it will bring to your soul and the time it frees up to invest in prayer.

CHAPTER 2

The Battle Over Time

Ilive in Lagos, Nigeria, and have done so for the past eight years. When my wife and I returned to live in Lagos in 2001, we chose to live in an enclosed residential area called Victoria Garden City. We were glad for the ambience it provided with two parks and a well-ordered environment very similar to Europe where we had lived in London for five years and before that in Copenhagen, Denmark, for one year as missionaries.

When we moved to Victoria Garden City, it took us, on average, 30 minutes during peak travel time to get to Victoria Island where our places of employment were located. Today it takes us, on average, two hours to make the same journey during peak travel time. The population increase in this part of the city quickly outstripped the road infrastructure. Consequently, we have had to make radical adjustments to our lifestyle to ensure we maintain our vital spiritual link to God in prayer. It was that serious!

The reality is that this is the challenge for many people worldwide. Longer work days, shorter vacations, and little job security. I know people who are afraid to leave their offices at the appointed closing hour for fear of offending their bosses who want to stay and work. I believe that travel and working conditions have become the 21st century challenge to spirituality.

Too often I have dived headlong into traffic without a moment's pause to pray. Morning prayer at home is far from my mind as I am consumed with making the traffic situation as painless as possible and getting to work on time where I have a myriad of issues to deal to with. These challenges are not peculiar to Lagos. Big city life anywhere can be demanding of our time. Is this story familiar?

I have adopted various strategies to help me overcome this challenge. Years ago when I was grappling with the demands of work, a new baby, and a long commute to work, I used my lunch hour to pray in a park near my office. I have also found great joy and strength from praying while spending hours in crawling traffic. Nevertheless, these are short-term strategies that cannot replace time purposefully spent in an unhurried manner in the presence of God.

The Enemy

The enemy understands that one precious ingredient we have is *time*. He also understands that time is a limited resource. It is different from eternal life in that God has apportioned a time limit to all that happens on earth. Solomon in Ecclesiastes said there is a time to every purpose under Heaven. Therefore our greatest battle on earth is over the utilization of time to enforce the will of God on earth. We don't have all of eternity to achieve this goal. If we had all the time in the world, Moses wouldn't have prayed to God to teach us to number our days that we may gain a heart of wisdom. It is this recognition of limited time that the enemy recognizes. The minute we recognize how limited and finite time is, our perspective of prayer, life, and productivity changes.

To limit or eliminate our proper utilization of time in prayer, the enemy ensures that the economic and social systems of the world keep us on a treadmill. The strategy is to keep us consumed with the business of work and career until we reach retirement age at which time we may be full of regret. Then we realize our unfulfilled potential in God or the fact that we never truly discovered our true purpose because we never took the time to be with Him.

The ultimate objective of the enemy is to make us impotent spiritually. This battle is not new, it has been fought in every generation. Many have lost, but some have equally won; and those who have won provide us illustrious company to which we must belong. The aim of the enemy's battle over time is to render us void of prayer. For when a man or woman is rendered void of prayer, impotence becomes the natural condition of such a person. One of the signs or symptoms of spiritual impotence in our day is what I call *spiritual anorexia*.

Spiritual Anorexia

Anorexia is a physical dysfunction that causes a person to lose appetite for food. It is dangerous and life threatening, and people who suffer this malady have to be treated specially. Now when this condition has a spiritual dimension, it translates to people without an appetite for spiritual things. This condition comes about due to prolonged periods of prayerlessness. It is now so widespread in the church that it has taken on the form of a plague. The single largest problem in the church is believers who have not embraced the culture of the Kingdom. They believe, but their lifestyle does not reflect what they believe—they live no differently from the world in the utilization of their time and their pursuits. So prolonged periods of prayerlessness due to the battle over our time causes chronic prayerlessness; and after a while, our desire for prayer disappears completely.

A quick test as to the existence of spiritual anorexia is whether we look forward to praying or find it a chore. Another sign: if given a choice, would we reach for the Bible or non-spiritual material to read? Yet another test is our attitude toward brothers and sisters in Christ who are different from us. Do we consider them irritants or are we compassionate and accommodating? To overcome in the 21st century, we must understand this strategy of the enemy.

It takes revelation and great effort to build an alternative lifestyle. For my wife and I, it first involved a reduction in income because we needed to reclaim our time. One day we reviewed our lifestyle and decided we needed to make radical adjustments. My wife realized that every Sunday evening, she would have the blues as Monday approached. The blues would descend like a cloud as the inevitability of the mad scramble faced us. Not only did we not have time to pray, we didn't have a sense of God's purpose either. We were caught up in the rat race. We saw that our one valuable resource—time—no longer belonged to us.

So my wife took a brave step and quit her job, much to the chagrin and shock of many. It was our way of heralding our deliverance. Then we had to depend on one income. This time in our lives had its financial challenges, but we were free to discover something better. The fear many of us harbor is a drop in income and it's effect on our lifestyle. What helped us, I must confess, was revelation. We trusted in the fact that as God's children we would discover a more meaningful and fruitful alternative to the rat race we were in.

This revelation came as we prayed for an alternative lifestyle. Our major discovery as we prayed was the fact that we had been contending with a system that sought to compete with our allegiance to God. An illustrative picture of what we had been facing was Daniel in Babylon at the time a decree was made banning prayer to God. This decree was actually engineered by some who were envious of Daniel's success and knew that if they could prevent him from praying, they would cut off his connection to God. Today we are faced with the same virulent agenda, only more subtle. It comes in the guise of work, career, and the corporate life, but ultimately it seeks to dethrone our allegiance to God.

Our Babylon

The system we confront is organized and seeks control and allegiance. It uses the seduction of material success as the bait to ensnare. The term the Bible uses to describe this system is "Babylon" or "mystery Babylon." In Revelation 18:3 Babylon's influence is described in these words:

For all the nations have drunk of the wine of the wrath of her fornication, the kings of the earth have committed fornication with her, and the merchants of the earth have become rich through the abundance of her luxury.

Our response to this seduction is deliverance and escape. Not a physical deliverance and escape as such (even though at times this is what is required), but a deliverance of the mind and the soul from the seductive hold of Babylon. This deliverance and escape is captured in the words of Revelation 18:4:

And I heard another voice from heaven saying, 'Come out of her, my people, lest you receive of her plagues.

The uncomfortable truth is most of us are ensnared by the material promises of Babylon and fail to see that Babylon's ultimate objective is to destroy our allegiance to God.

This snare has become even more deadly because many believers cannot distinguish between godly prosperity and covetousness. They are different even though the outward appearance of either may look the same. Just as two men wear suits and you can't tell the character of either until you weigh their actions and their words, so also is the difference between godly prosperity and covetousness. Many have succumbed to covetousness in the deluded belief that it was godly prosperity because of an inordinate desire for the perceived trappings of success. Believers in the workplace see their jobs as the primary source of material acquisition and advancement. So even when the workplace is making ungodly demands on our time, we believe it is a sacrifice to be made in order to acquire the trappings of success.

When Jesus was about to commence His work on earth, the devil deployed much the same strategy in these words captured by Matthew's account in chapter 4, verse 9, "All these things I will give You if You will fall down and worship me." Without a doubt the devil's chief objective was to truncate Jesus' mission on earth and destroy His allegiance to God. Now if the devil thought it fit to tempt Jesus probably knowing the predictable outcome, how much more us? Clearly, therefore, he unleashes his arsenal against us in the hope that our destiny will be truncated. Every believer needs to confront this devilish agenda!

DANIEL'S LESSONS

Daniel was very conscious of the importance of time and how it related to the affairs of his day. Therefore the Book of Daniel has many instructive lessons about this battle and the actions we must take to overturn the schemes and wiles of the devil. We can observe from Daniel's life that his rise to prominence was a product of his devotion to God. When Daniel was first confronted with the king's menu, he chose a lean diet, choosing a meal that kept him lean, alert, and sensitive to the ways of God. His stance was radically different from the norm of his day. When faced with the threat of death because Nebuchadnezzar wanted an interpretation of a dream, which no one knew, it was in God's presence that the contents of the dream and their interpretation came. Daniel knew how vitally important it was to stay connected. This link ensured that not only did he become a great administrator, excelling before different kings, he stood out as a prophetic voice of God in his day and beyond.

It was as a result of Daniel's spiritual success fundamentally that the enemy sought to go for the jugular by seeking to cut off his connection to God. When the ruling elite in Daniel's day saw they could not fault him in any way other than his allegiance to God, they ensured a law was passed banning prayer. Of all things to ban, it was prayer; and so the battle lines were drawn as the penalty for disobedience was death.

> So the governors and satraps sought to find some charge against Daniel concerning the kingdom: but they could find no charge or fault, because he was faithful; nor was there any error or fault found in him. Then these men said, "We shall not find any charge against this Daniel unless we find it against him concerning the law of his God" (Daniel 6:4-5).

After the law was passed, Daniel literally took his life in his hands by opposing the law in very strong terms.

> *Now when Daniel knew that the writing was signed, he went home. And in his upper room, with his **windows open** toward Jerusalem, he knelt down on his knees three times that day, and prayed and gave thanks before his God, as was his custom since early days. Then these men assembled and found Daniel praying and making supplication before his God. And they went before the king, and spoke concerning the king's decree: "Have you not signed a decree that every man who petitions any god or man within thirty days, except you, O king shall be cast into the den of lions?"* (Daniel 6:10-12)

Note that Daniel's weapon of confrontation was his *prayer and supplication* to God on his knees. Daniel broke the power of this law in prayer. Daniel understood that the law was intended to neutralize him spiritually, and he fought the best way he knew—on his knees! Daniel could have avoided this battle to save his life, but rather he confronted it head-on and obtained victory, completely annihilating the enemy.

This battle is vicious because it has to do with the purposes of God ordained for specific times and seasons. The fundamentals of this war are to truncate the purpose of God in the season for fulfillment. Our strategy ought not to be different from Daniel's strategy. When the enemy seeks to neutralize us, we should rather confront the issue head-on by doing everything necessary to safeguard our prayer link to God. We don't win by avoiding battle. When we avoid the battle or pretend it doesn't exist, we lose sight of the fact that the enemy's ultimate objective is to render us impotent. No job, career, or business is so important as to render us spiritually impotent in this life. Tragically, this is the option many have chosen out of ignorance.

In Daniel 7:25 the Bible records that, "He shall speak pompous words against the Most High, shall persecute the saints of the Most High, and shall intend to change times and law...." We see that the strategy of the devil is not only to persecute the saints but also to seek to change times and seasons. I believe what he seeks to change are spiritual times and seasons so that we live as though our lives don't have any spiritual context. In other words, he wants us living without the recognition that every believer has specific assignments allotted to us by God to be accomplished within a specific time frame.

Like Daniel, the only antidote we have is prayer. Our spiritual windows must be open to Jerusalem. This is the only antidote. I challenge you to start a deliverance project, to deliver yourself from the clutches of Babylon. I guarantee you that you will soon find the real you as you press into destiny in the place of prayer.

FASTING AND PRAYER

On another occasion, Daniel was fasting and praying over a 21-day period regarding a message he had received during the reign of Cyrus, King of Persia. Then an angel said to Daniel:

> *Do not fear, Daniel, for from the first day that you set your heart to understand, and to humble yourself before your God, your words were heard; and I have come because of your words. But behold the prince of the kingdom of Persia withstood me twenty-one days; and behold, Michael, one of the chief princes, came to help me, for I had been left alone there with the kings of Persia* (Daniel 10:12-13).

Notice that from this story, the angel sent in response to Daniel's prayer was resisted by the prince of Persia for 21 days in order to prevent him from going to Daniel with the answer to Daniel's prayer. So for the entire time Daniel prayed, the prince of Persia resisted him, so to speak. The angel told Daniel that from the first day you prayed, your words were heard. However, though Daniel was heard on the first day, the response did not come for another 21 days. Why did the prince of Persia resist Daniel? It was because he hoped that Daniel would relent in seeking God. Thankfully Daniel did not relent but persevered. It was this unrelenting, persevering partnership involving Daniel on earth and the God of the heavens and the earth that ensured that archangel Michael, one of the chief princes, went to help the angel on assignment. The battle over time and ultimately over divine purpose is intense. We must be confrontational and unrelenting as we pray.

Prayer, therefore, is nonnegotiable. Prayer allows us to fight the war raging over our destinies. Prayer helps us to stay strong and resist discouragement despite the pompous words the enemy speaks against us and the spread of God's dominion. Unfortunately, many are ignorant of the grand schemes of the enemy. Don't let your circumstances stand in the way of God's purpose for your life. If you can't find the time, *make* the time—especially if you find yourself constantly isolated from prayer. If you find yourself regularly isolated from prayer, you will need to take radical steps to turn things around. For instance, you may find it useful to deny yourself sleep just to break the cycle of prayerlessness. Whatever the price, we must pay that price to get the victory ordained by God.

CHAPTER 3

Prayer Culture

So He himself often withdrew into the wilderness and prayed
(Luke 5:16).

I can't imagine anyone who hasn't struggled with balancing the demands of everyday life with the need to pray. This is an area in which we all struggle, whether a pastor, business person, stay-at-home parent, corporate CEO, or mechanic. When I first got serious in my relationship with Jesus, I used a daily devotional titled "Every Day With Jesus," written by the late Selwyn Hughes. At the time, I was a young, upwardly mobile lawyer. This meant that sometimes I would be in court and at other times I would be meeting deadlines as I drafted various commercial agreements. My excuse many times for not praying consistently was my job.

Then a few years later, I was overseeing a church in Denmark and you would imagine that the nature of what I was doing would mean that praying daily would be easier. I found to my surprise that it wasn't so. I soon realized that cultivating the right habits involved hard work and discipline.

This realization didn't necessarily make it easier. There were times, for instance, when I would wake up early but find myself stuck to the bed especially in the cold, wintry months in Denmark when the temperature would stay in the minus range for months. On some days I would jump out of bed, start brewing some coffee, and jump back in bed emerging only after I could smell the aroma of the coffee. On other days I would pray with a friend of mine who faithfully arrived at my flat every Monday morning to pray. And of course there were many occasions when I would look out of the window and see him and want to pretend I wasn't home. But I kept at it.

Recently some friends and I have prayed together every morning for the past year. And even now there are many mornings when I have no desire whatsoever to pray. It takes discipline to will myself out of the bed.

What has kept me going is the fact that I am doing what Jesus did on a regular basis. If Jesus did it, then this is something I need to do also. The Scriptures about Jesus' attitude about prayer lights up with revelation. Who would believe that Jesus, the sinless, perfect Son of God, would need to pray! If Jesus needed that vital connection with God regularly, then the least I can do is imitate Him. If Jesus could find time to pray irrespective of how busy He was, then I certainly have no excuse.

I have often read and re-read the account of Jesus having the presence of mind to seek a solitary place to pray after spending the night before teaching the multitude, healing all who were sick, and casting out many demons. What amazing presence of mind! He successfully resisted the temptation that plagues us daily—the snare of *being busy*.

Many times I have been very diligent to pray when I am desperate for God to solve a problem or see me through a difficult phase only to fall back to old habits of prayerlessness as soon as the difficulty is over. I know this challenge is not limited to me. Many of us remember to pray only when problems are upon us. As if this were not bad enough, when success and public acclaim come, they come with all the accompanying perks, habits, and lifestyles programmed to crowd out God. At times like this, prayer becomes short, dignified, and cursory.

I know many pastors, business people, and politicians who are ensnared by the perception of being busy to their spiritual detriment. Have you ever wondered how sometimes a high-profile, well-respected pastor suddenly announces that he has commenced divorce proceedings? Usually the painful tragedy is a result of success and its perks taking center stage in that person's life to the detriment of the first principles of prayer.

God has ordained life to work by fixed principles. When we apply the fixed principles of God to how we live daily, life becomes predictable. God never intends that any of us should suffer shipwreck or failure in life. If it were so, God would be unjust. This is why even if someone doesn't have a relationship with God based on the redeeming work of Jesus Christ, but nevertheless applies the principles of God, they have success. How much more then for those to whom the invitation is available to have eternal life and enjoy the privilege of being the offspring of the most high God?

The joy of prayer as we make progress through the different stages of life is that it helps retain our connection to God's heart. It helps keep our focus on what our treasure is. Jesus said where your treasure is, determines where your heart will be (see Matt. 6:21). So our journey through the different stages of life presents us with the challenge of the many things that want to ensnare our soul, but prayer keeps our heart on God. This in turn ensures that our internal compass is providing accurate direction, bringing us farther and farther into the perfect will of God.

MARKETPLACE PRAYER

A few years ago, I was one of the founding partners of a thriving law firm in Lagos. Fortunately, my partners and I shared a common belief in the central importance of prayer. And so every Tuesday from 7-9 in the morning we would pray. It was tough many times because very often there were compelling reasons, or so they seemed, why we should shelve our praying and do something more "meaningful." We had deadlines to meet on a regular basis, and sometimes clients wanted to meet with us at that time. On other occasions, we were faced with the need to travel for meetings outside Lagos. Yet we wanted to maintain this culture of prayer. We wanted to show that, in addition to being lawyers, we were priests in the marketplace as well.

We were determined to be different. We wanted the reality of the Kingdom of God to be evident in all that we did. So we persevered; and each time we met to pray, our prayer touched many different subjects. Sometimes we simply interceded for our staff. Other times we prayed about our business and the challenges we were facing. Other times we prayed about our profession. Yet at other times we also prayed for the country and its leadership. The discipline of praying regularly every week had many benefits. As partners, we never had disagreements we were not able to resolve. As partners, we had revelation about the foundation of the supernatural realm of God influencing and impacting all our actions, decisions, choices, and strategies. We were also reminded of Jesus' attitude to public acclaim, acutely aware that success could be a snare even though it ought not to be so.

We had many stories to tell of the miraculous favor of God as we prayed. Therefore we declared it an office policy and made every effort to get together on Tuesdays to pray. We wanted to imitate Jesus who maintained His focus on prayer as a lifestyle regardless of public acclaim. He never got carried away. So even though the report of the miracles went around concerning Him and great multitudes thronged to hear Him, Jesus often withdrew into the wilderness and prayed.

Apart from experiencing the favor of God, we also took time to pray and deal with certain challenges we faced in our profession such as corruption. On one occasion, we prayed about the demands for bribe from a certain business for whom we had done legal work. As we prayed, we sensed a stirring in our hearts to pray for the removal of a certain person from a position of authority because the person had become a stumbling block demanding that if we didn't pay a bribe we would be frustrated in collecting our duly earned fees. About three weeks after we prayed, the person was removed from that position. What a reassuring way to be reminded about the indispensable culture of prayer.

Jesus Prayed

Jesus' prayers were not irregular forays born of fits of revelation or occasional bursts of energy—rather they were a regular habit He practiced because His visits to the wilderness to pray occurred often. The transforming power of prayer comes through a lifestyle of praying often. This requires discipline. Many times we want to run away from the demands of discipline. But discipline is the key. Discipline is a habit we must establish, no matter the cost. Without discipline we will never get the best out of our relationship with God. This is what we learn from the lifestyle of Jesus.

Without discipline we cannot get the best out of the spiritual realm. Our vital connection to God is spiritual; and therefore, we need discipline to ensure we overcome the distractions of the world and regularly maintain our link with God. Too often we seek prayer as an emergency mantra to ward off evil or reverse our fortunes for the better. However, prayer is an intimate activity with a divine personality. As such, we often seek Him because He has a will over every aspect of human existence.

Jesus recognized that the key to being fruitful in every area of life was consistency in His connection to God in prayer. Over the years I had struggled with the idea of consistency because I thought it was impossible to maintain daily consistency in prayer. I thought that in Jesus' day the economies were agrarian and therefore praying early in the morning before heading off to the farm would be natural; while modern-day, big city realities denied one such an option. But whenever I have attempted consistency, I have found the benefits to be tremendous!

About a year ago, a friend of mine and I decided to embark on a daily prayer project together. We decided to pray every morning without fail from 5 until 7. When my friend moved to another neighborhood a couple of months later, we moved the time by an hour. Even though we expected great results, we were amazed at the range and scale of the impact of our prayers. No matter the cost, I assure you there is no other way to get the best in your relationship with God.

Prayer is so important that when it comes to making job decisions, we should beware of jobs that may offer mouthwatering salaries, yet keep us enslaved to work such that we have no time to pray. It is important to find jobs that allow us to maintain our relationship with God. I have friends, for instance, who found themselves enslaved to work that gave no room for anything; they left those jobs in order to restore a proper work life balance. I am not advocating that we hide under the need to pray as a reason for not being gainfully employed—this would be unscriptural since the Bible says he who would not work should also not eat (see 2 Thess. 3:10). What I am advocating is the boldness to take radical steps to ensure that we get the best out of our relationship with God.

The first amazing impact from our daily early morning prayer sessions was the way it began to change us. We were more accommodating, patient, compassionate, sensitive to others, and above all more loving. When previous hurts and offenses reared their heads, we prayed for those who had spitefully treated us, just as Jesus commanded we do.

The next amazing thing, it was easier for us to discern what God would have us pray about. We became so much more aware of the heart of God and of His will. In fact, we began to feel as though we had been backslidden for years previous.

Third, our prayer time stirred a deep hunger for His Word, and not just reading it, but studying and seeking to really understand the heart of God. It made relationships and ministry so much easier to cope with because we were beginning to connect with a deeper dimension of grace.

As I write, we have not set an end date to this prayer project. We trust that God will continue to lead us and enliven our time together by His Spirit.

PRACTICAL STEPS TO EFFECTIVE PRAYING

I want to share some practical lessons I have learned over the years that helped me tremendously in developing a lifestyle of prayer. I do this to demystify prayer. I feel many people have come to the conclusion that consistent prayer is not for everyone. What a sad conclusion that is! I also know many who consider the emphasis some of us have placed on prayer as being "overly spiritual." This is another unfortunate conclusion. Yet others feel we go on about prayer so much so that we are on the verge of losing sight of the grace of God. I understand all these perceptions because I have discussed them often with many friends of mine. I believe it is important to share personal, practical experiences. What follows will throw light on this all-important subject.

Determine Priorities

The first practical step is for us to determine what our *priorities* are. This may seem obvious enough as many of us have a sense of our priorities. But if we take time to really think about them, we may discover that our priorities are not what we confess. To truly understand our priorities requires reflection. Our reflections will lead us to the pattern we see in our lives, which will in turn lead us to analyze how we spend our time. The activities that take up our time more often than not are the activities we have placed a premium on.

I find many people who struggle with the idea of a life devoted to prayer haven't addressed this fundamental issue. Many of us undoubtedly believe in Jesus Christ and have accepted His sacrifice as the price that brought us reconciliation with our Father in Heaven, but we haven't found the roadmap to an enduring relationship with our Father. So we search for all kinds of props and end up filling our lives with secondary material such as church meetings, books, conventions, seminars, and our favorite television ministries and pastors.

Consistent prayer seems alien because spending regular time with God has become like making friends with a stranger on his own terms. Many of us find that when the chips are down, God takes second place in our lives. Competing for our hearts many times are our jobs, family, business, etc. Remember, Jesus said, "Where your treasure is, there your heart will be also" (Matt. 6:21). Our treasure is far from God even though we confess Him as Lord. Our first step must be to address the challenge Jesus threw to everyone following Him. These are His words in Luke 14:26:

> If anyone comes to Me and does not hate his father and mother, wife and children, brothers and sisters, yes, and his own life also, he cannot be My disciple.

In other words, Jesus expects total devotion. Nothing is expected to compete with our devotion to Him. This should cause us some reflection. Christianity is an invitation to a radical lifestyle that is totally at odds with the world. It runs counter to every principle of the world. So our first task is to determine what really matters to us. When we do so, we are keenly sensitive about how we spend our time. Certain habits we soon discover are counterproductive.

For instance, when I realized that I had to be consistent in prayer some things had to give way. Late night movies had to go because they had a negative effect on my ability to wake up early to pray. Furthermore, I discovered that my temperament suited for praying in the mornings depended on how I spent the night before.

If we don't address these issues, we would never truly succeed in discovering the correct lifestyle. In a world where so much is competing for our attention, lifestyle adjustments are the great demand of the 21st century. We will need to reexamine the habits and lifestyles we have come to accept as normal. I know many families who invest heavily in vacations abroad, traveling to many exotic destinations sometimes twice and three times a year—yet have never invested in developing a prayer life. And they are believers! Too many of us want to live like the world but at the same time be assured of our passport to Heaven. We forget that it is impossible to serve two masters. We either hate one or love the other (see Matt. 6:24).

Time Management

After we determine what really matters to us, the next important step is *time management*. Consistency doesn't come because we wish it. It comes because we make time available each day. We have to allot a specific time. This may be in the morning or in the evening or even during the day, depending on our responsibilities. If we don't make the time available, there will always be something competing for that time. We must do whatever is necessary to ensure we keep to that time.

But you may say what about the grace of God. I would say the grace of God never negates discipline. Rather it assures us of the availability of God's grace to make us disciplined. For instance, I pray with some friends every morning and we have done this now for over 18 months. When we started we didn't believe we could maintain consistency for this length of time. Against all our expectations it has lasted more than a year. This for me is the grace of God. Not grace to cover up for my laziness but grace to help me do what I don't like doing.

However, some who started praying with us have not been able to stay consistent for all sorts of reasons. The main reason has been because they hadn't planned and set aside the time, so other things demanded that time. Whether we like it or not, there are many things waiting to make a demand on our time. From the moment we are awake, the demand on our time begins. It maybe the urgency of phone calls, text messages, our spouses, children, work, church activities, friends, etc.

Jesus understood the need for great discipline. He is the example per excellence of the disciplined life:

> *And He said to them, "come aside by yourselves to a deserted place and rest a while." For there were many coming and going, and they did not even have time to eat. So they departed to a deserted place in the boat by themselves. But the multitudes saw them departing, and many knew Him and ran there on foot from all the cities. They arrived before them and together to Him. And Jesus, when He came out, saw a*

great multitude and was moved with compassion for them, because they were like sheep not having a shepherd. So He began to teach them many things. When the day was now far spent, His disciples came to Him and said, "this is a deserted place, and already the hour is late. Send them away, that they might go into the surrounding country and villages and buy themselves bread; for they have nothing to eat." But He answered and said to them, "You give them something to eat." ...So they all ate and were filled. ...He sent the multitudes away. And when He had sent them away, He departed to the mountain to pray (Mark 6:31-46).

There are many things we can learn from this story in the Book of Mark, but I focus on Jesus' departure to the mountain to pray. This story starts with Jesus' invitation to the disciples to come away from the hustle and bustle to pray. This initial effort was thwarted by the multitudes that followed Jesus in droves. Nevertheless, Jesus took time away from His original goal to feed them spiritually and physically. When He was finished, He went back to what had been on His mind all along. *He departed to the mountain to pray.* This for me is one of the greatest examples of discipline. Jesus had lost time because His original intention was to go away to a deserted place with His disciples. He met the needs of the people who gathered to Him. When He was finished, He went up to the mountain to pray. At times like this we must jealously protect the time we have set aside.

Retreat to a Deserted Place

From Jesus' example we also discover that another great habit is to cultivate the lifestyle of regular times away from the hustle and bustle of life. The rewards of doing this are extremely far-reaching. The key again is setting aside time to do this on a regular basis. I started going on retreats on a regular basis in 2005. Prior to this time I had been on retreats sporadically. I was greatly inspired by the lifestyle of Pastor Sunday Adelaja based in Ukraine. I heard him say that he had gone away on retreats for a week, every month, and that he had done this consistently for the past ten years. When I heard this, I was greatly inspired to seek God like never before.

When I go on retreats they are personally transforming. I come back changed. I am less aggravated by problems; I am calmer. At home I am a better husband and father. I display more fruit of the Holy Spirit. I have greater clarity concerning what God would have me do. I receive wisdom to deal with thorny issues. I would normally go away for three days at a time.

The truth is, though, when the time comes to go away, it is as though all hell breaks loose. Problems needing my attention crop up. At other times someone would fall ill in my home. One of the most interesting times was when my business partners and I were to meet with a minister in government. The day of the meeting clashed with the day I had set aside to go on a retreat. I was in a dilemma. I had fixed the dates of the retreat before we were given the appointment with the minister. I was also concerned that my partners would consider me fanatical if I went ahead with my retreat because this was someone very important and it had taken some time and effort to get the appointment.

I asked God what to do in the circumstances. The Lord wouldn't let me off the hook, and so I returned to my partners and they kindly agreed to attend the meeting without me. However, while they were arriving for the meeting, the minister was called away to another meeting and so my partners could not meet with him. The meeting was rescheduled for another date and we all attended the meeting and had a very useful and instructive discussion with the minister. I learned very quickly from that experience to stand my ground and put God first.

When you determine to take this practical step, there will be much opposition. Sometimes the opposition will be glaring and at other times it will be subtle, because the enemy loathes it when we determine to seek God.

Building Prayer Partnerships

Finally, I have learned from my experience that it is also vital to find friends who share a passion to pray. This is because discouragement comes especially when it seems as though God is not answering your prayer. This is when you need friends who will inspire you. You will be amazed at the strength you can receive when praying with a friend when you are personally weary.

Many people suffer unnecessary spiritual burnout because they haven't discovered the joy of having friends and family with whom to pray on a consistent basis. Years ago in Denmark I had a Danish friend who would come unfailingly every Monday to my home to pray. Most times we prayed about the country. In the winter months, I struggled a great deal to make our Monday morning meetings; but because the meetings were held in my home, I could not escape them. And this guy, without fail, would be at my home irrespective of how cold it was. I remember one occasion when he arrived on his bicycle on a day when the snow that had fallen the previous night made it difficult for even cars to move—yet this guy was at my door ringing the bell.

In the past ten years I have gathered with many different sets of friends at various times to pray. The aim has been to help each other maintain consistency in prayer. We may start off in one home and pray for four weeks or thereabouts. Then we change location and somebody else volunteers his or her home. This helps us maintain some freshness and commitment to each other. More recently, I again have friends who are especially focused in consistent praying such that it again inspires me to dig deeper to discover what God has in store.

It is vital to be true to yourself. Don't pretend your priority is God because it is the proper thing to think. Be honest with yourself and begin the journey of discovering your real priorities. The worst thing you can do is deceive yourself. All around the world today, most people seek God for what they can get. This has always been true of all human beings since the world began. God spoke through Jeremiah the prophet and it was a lamentation. He said:

> ...My people have committed two evils; they have forsaken Me, the fountain of living waters, and have hewn

for themselves cisterns—broken cisterns that can hold no water (Jeremiah 2:13).

In other words, God's lament through Jeremiah was that of an abandoned Father. So many of us have forsaken God in pursuit of what we can get. When God gets serious and demands fruit, many leave because we are not ready for the attentive demands of a Father.

Jesus said to the disciples:

> *Whoever eats My flesh and drinks My blood has eternal life, and I will raise him up at the last day. For My flesh is food indeed, and My blood is drink indeed. He who eats My flesh and drinks My blood abides in Me, and I in Him. As the living Father sent Me, and I live because of the Father, so he who feeds on Me will live because of Me. ...Therefore many of His disciples, when they heard this, said, "This is a hard saying; who can understand it?"* (John 6:54-60)

Many disciples couldn't stomach this saying and left Jesus. This has been the challenge of Christianity through the ages. At every point in our journey we must check that God is truly our priority. These guys who left were not the multitude content with the miracles, healings, and teachings of Jesus. These guys were described as disciples, which meant they had experienced a deeper measure of life with Jesus. Yet their thoughts were that this was a *hard saying; who can understand it.* So rather than seek understanding, they departed. What a tragedy!

But would you believe many of us leave Jesus at the point where He is demanding a deeper level of consecration and surrender to His will? Many of us suddenly realize when the chips are down that what we really wanted from Him was just what He could give us. When Jesus is your priority, one of the first things that happens is that you stop struggling to prove a point.

Many of us, especially pastors, are caught up in a frenzy to prove that our church is on the cutting edge; that it has the best worship team; the best worship center, etc. All these are nothing but vanity. When Jesus is our priority, every ambition fades away and all we want to do is find practical ways to invest our time in our relationship with Him and play our role in transforming our world for Him.

Whatever you do, make God your priority.

CHAPTER 4

Prophetic Wombs of Destiny

This day is a day of trouble and rebuke and blasphemy; for the children have come to birth, but there is no strength to bring them forth (Isaiah 37:3).

...This is a black day. We're like pregnant women without even the strength to have a baby... (Isaiah 37:3 MSG).

"Before she was in labor, she gave birth; before her pain came, she delivered a male child. Who has heard such a thing? Who has seen such things? Shall the earth be made to give birth in one day? Or shall a nation be born at once? For as soon as Zion was in labor, she gave birth to her children. Shall I bring to the time of birth, and not cause delivery?" says the Lord. *"Shall I who cause delivery shut up the womb?"* says your God (Isaiah 66:7-9).

These Scriptures paint a prophetic picture of the choice we face as members of the Body of Christ seeking to fulfill His purpose. Each of us has unique gifts and abilities given to us by God with the objective of carrying out different assignments that in one way or another reconcile, disciple, and commission men and women to advance the Kingdom of God on earth. As we discover these assignments, we find out that they are like burdens within us waiting to come forth. In other words, they are like children waiting to be born at an appointed time.

From Isaiah 37:3 we receive the first illustration:

> *This day is a day of trouble and rebuke and blasphemy; for the children have come to birth, but there is no strength to bring forth* (Isaiah 37:3).

The appointed time had come when the new breed of Judah was to have been born but there was no strength to labor and give birth. So here was Hezekiah faced with the frustration of a lack of strength to take Judah to the next level. The background to this illustration is found in Isaiah's account of the planned siege of Judah. Sennacherib, the King of Syria, sent the Rabshakeh (chief of staff or governor) with an army to besiege Judah. When news of the plan reached Hezekiah, he sent word to Isaiah the prophet. Hezekiah's words were words of lamentation. Hezekiah was lamenting the powerlessness of Judah in the face of the impending siege by the Syrian forces. Hezekiah was also lamenting the pompous words, which Sennacherib had spoken about the certainty of Syria's victory over Judah. So he likened their condition to that of a pregnant woman who doesn't have the strength to go through with labor. The Message translation puts it succinctly: *"we're like pregnant women without even the strength to have a baby."*

Hezekiah was probably at a deeper level also lamenting the fact that going by the words spoken by the Rabshakeh, the Lord was now perceived as no different from the idols of the nations that surrounded Judah because of Judah's idolatrous ways. In Isaiah 36:7 the Rabshakeh said:

> *But if you say to me, "we trust in the Lord our God" is it not He whose high places and whose altars Hezekiah has taken away and said to Judah and Jerusalem, "you shall worship before this altar?"*

Hezekiah was a reforming king who sought to reestablish the worship of God in Judah. At the time he ascended the throne, Judah had become so steeped in idolatry that even its neighbors like Syria could no longer distinguish the worship of God from the worship of Baal. Therefore when Hezekiah was cleansing the land of its idolatry, outsiders like Sennacherib had no clue as to what was going on. Rather, he thought Hezekiah was doing Judah grave harm, not recognizing that he was restoring the nation back to the one true God!

BAD TIMES

This is how bad things were in Judah when Hezekiah ascended the throne. The people of Judah no longer worshiped God. The temple was locked up, and the people had succumbed to all kinds of idolatrous practices, which they had learned from the surrounding nations. In the first year of his reign, Hezekiah gave this command to the people of Judah:

> *"Hear me Levites! Now sanctify yourselves, sanctify the house of the Lord God of your fathers, and carry out the rubbish from the holy place"* (2 Chronicles 29:5).

Hezekiah was determined to reintroduce the God of Abraham, Isaac, and Jacob to the people of Judah. What Hezekiah set out to do was so radical and unprecedented because the people of Judah no longer had God as the centerpiece of their lives. To understand how bad it was, the envoy Sennacherib sent to Hezekiah could boast in these words:

> *Thus says the King: "Do not let Hezekiah deceive you, for he will not be able to deliver you; nor let Hezekiah make you trust in the Lord, saying 'the Lord will surely deliver us...'"* (Isaiah 36:14-15).

Further on the envoy would also say, "Beware lest Hezekiah persuade you, saying, 'The Lord will deliver us.' Has any of the gods of the nations delivered its land from the king of Assyria?" (Isa. 36:18). This was the state of affairs in the nation of Judah! The knowledge of God was so poor that God was seen as no different from the other gods or idols worshiped by people whom the Assyrians had conquered. So when Hezekiah sent word to Isaiah saying, "It's a day of rebuke and blasphemy when the children come to birth and there is no strength to bring forth," he was expressing his pain at the mockery Judah had become to a heathen nation like Assyria. He recognized that the reformation, which had begun in Judah, was critically also about the strength to give "birth" to a new kind of people—the "children of destiny." The king of Assyria was the face of opposition to the birthing process. Hezekiah recognized that the critical factor in the unfolding drama was strength to give birth. He had to stay focused on his unique assignment of bringing the nation back to God.

BIRTHING THE CHURCH

This story is also illustrative of the condition of the church today. As in Hezekiah's day, the ways of the church are so indistinguishable from the ways of the world such that when a sweeping reformation begins, many will think the reformation is working against God's purpose. We are so steeped in the culture of the world on many fronts that a return to our true origins will to many look like a destruction of the very essence of church.

For instance, when churches truly begin to prepare and equip men and women for the works of their ministry and pastors lose the centralized control of what is considered "my vision," the unfolding character of church will be different from what it is today. For a start, the liberation from the pews coupled with a loss of centralized control will change the nature of assemblies. The focus on church membership numbers as a reference point, especially in one location, will become irrelevant. The church will become more diffused, more infiltrative, and its reach will be greater across the nations of the earth.

Hezekiah's lament, therefore, was the lament of an unfinished reformation business faced with the threat of its truncation by Sennacherib, king of Syria. Hezekiah hadn't gotten around to building. The new breed had not yet come forth. The business of reformation was incomplete and it was in this state of unfinished business that the threat of Syria presented itself.

On the other hand, the picture presented by Isaiah 66:7-9 is very different. What we see is a picture of the imminence of delivery. Birth is assured. From the moment that labor was imminent, there was an assurance of delivery. Before birth pains came, delivery was assured and so even the prophet exclaimed, "*Who has heard such a thing? Who has seen such things?*"

So whereas Hezekiah illustrates for us the frustration of an unfinished transition from idolatry to true worship, the prophet Isaiah illustrates for us in Isaiah 66 the power of God to bring forth what He has ordained at an appointed time. What do we learn from this? We learn to first discern the prophetic times in which we live and our appropriate response to these times.

In God's prophetic timetable, more than ever before, we live in a time when the groan of creation waiting for the manifestation of the sons of God is rising to a crescendo. There are two options before us. Do we wallow in frustration because we are still grappling with the transition from the current idolatry of the church such that we are unable to give birth to or release the children of destiny who will meet the needs of creation? Or do we sense that the seasons have changed! For indeed the season *has* changed. The season of powerlessness is over and a season of acceleration is here.

The accumulation of prophetic pronouncements over the church bringing direction regarding what the church should be in the 21st century coupled with the unfinished global apostolic transition seeking to exemplify what this reformation should be like has caused deep frustration for today's reformers who desire to see the children of destiny born to fulfill God's mandate, which is yet to take place. In the midst of this frustration, God has released a new grace to give birth because the whole of creation groans waiting for the manifestation of the sons of God. These sons are shaking off the frustration of incomplete transitions. They are embracing a new grace to come forth with the purpose of God. Every son and daughter must give birth to the destiny ordained by God for each of them at this appointed time.

LABOR AND BIRTH

The idea of laboring to give birth is something I have experienced repeatedly. The first time I vividly remember having a personal experience of giving birth was in December 1994 in Lagos. I had just come through a traumatic season in my life. It was my first experience of ministry after which I found myself unceremoniously replaced. I was despondent and at a crossroads regarding what next to do. About this time three friends and I headed off to a friend's country home in Epe, a coastal town approximately an hour's drive from Lagos, to spend some time praying. We were so desperate for change because as it turned out we were all at very defining moments in our lives. I needed to know what was in store for me in the next season of my life.

One of my friends had just left his job as an engineering consultant and was taking over from me in my previous ministry role. Another friend had just returned from London where he just had his first experience as a pastor of a church outside Nigeria and was then in the process of obtaining the appropriate travel documents. My third friend was seeking to carve his own niche in business, coming out from under the shadows of his father who was already a very successful businessman. We set aside three days to pray and fast. In doing so we were all keenly aware that our coming together to pray would give birth to God's will for the next season of our lives.

I was faced with many choices. I could succumb to bitterness, regret, self-pity, and depression, or shake myself free from the pain and anger of the moment and give birth to something new. I am eternally grateful to God that I chose the latter. For the three days we were away, we denied ourselves food and spent an average of six hours praying every day.

This may sound incredible because you may be wondering what we said in the six hours we spent praying and how we found the strength to pray that long considering we were denying ourselves food. For much of the time, we prayed in diverse tongues. (I describe the limitless treasures available to every one who prays in tongues in the next chapter.) By the time we came away from the retreat, we were certain that we had given birth spiritually. Within six months of that time together, each of us was in a different part of the world doing different things all for the advance of the Kingdom. I went off to Denmark to pastor a new church. Armed with the revelation of the power to give birth to divine purpose, I arrived in Denmark with a passion to disciple fellow believers to discover their spiritual womb in the place of prayer. Another friend went off to London and today leads one of the most influential churches in the city. The one who succeeded me in my old ministry role went to Germany eventually and today speaks flawless German. He is driven by a passion to penetrate German culture in order to effectively and positively bring the gospel of the Kingdom of God to Germans. It was truly an amazing experience to give birth to purpose as we prayed.

MOVING FORWARD

What choices do you face today and what actions will you take? The point is we cannot choose the circumstances of life that confront us; however, we can choose what we make of the circumstances. Don't moan and groan about the challenges you face. Rise up in faith and expectation *"for as soon as Zion was in labor, she gave birth to her children."* Today there is grace to give birth to purpose. Who knows what great destiny awaits you as you come before God to give birth to divine purpose. Every season must be approached with great expectation that as we labor and travail in prayer we will give birth to divine purpose.

The tragedy—many of us succumb to pain and bitterness and the wounds of offense. When this happens, it cripples our ability to move forward.

Approximately six or seven years later, I would be at another crossroads about my future. Should I remain in the United Kingdom or should I return to Nigeria? I yearned for a new lease on life, but the challenges seemed insurmountable. The UK had become my comfort zone. We had a nice home, and our two young sons were enjoying growing up in a stable, middle-class suburb of London. Even though I was attempting to find a new rhythm for myself, my wife had a good job and there was no compelling reason to move except, of course, for the fact that I had a yearning that wouldn't go away. In addition, a couple of years earlier I had thought about relocating and had written in my journal my impression of God's view of the matter, which came across to me as "not yet time." A few years later I could clearly sense a resonance in my spirit declaring that it was time. So this time my wife and I would embark on the birthing process together. We would return to Nigeria, where we currently live, and start a new phase of life.

I have discovered an important principle of life—God ordains a thing but requires me to take ownership of it and birth it in the place of prayer. Prayer then becomes the divine energy required to force the "baby" of destiny from the womb of the spirit realm into reality. It requires desperation, hunger, frustration, and whatever else that would cause us to travail until quite literally we sense something has been born in the spirit realm.

For me at the time, the trigger was being jolted out of my previous position unceremoniously! It requires a tenacity to stay focused until it happens. This birthing process may take a few minutes or it may take days or months of travail. The reason many never press into the purposes of God, even after they have heard prophecies spoken, is because they don't recognize that every prophecy causes conceptualization in the womb of destiny. But when the appointed time for birthing comes, it requires tenacity and travail to bring forth what God had prophesied. It is for reasons of birthing that God gives us the gift of diversity of tongues and groaning in the spirit. When the time of birthing comes, our desire will release new tongues, which we may never have spoken before.

In addition, a groan may begin to well up from deep within us. It is the travail of birthing. At times like these, something great is about to happen! We must continue with fervency, joy, and faith knowing that something tangible and life-transforming is coming forth. It is this kind of travail that causes Isaiah in chapter 54 to ask the barren to rejoice because as a result of her travail she will give birth to more than the woman who has and there will be the extending of her borders as she expands on every side. These are spiritual realities that we experience by the awesome grace of God.

By the Grace of God

I have found from experience that the times when I have been faced with the need to give birth to purpose, a new season in my life, a business project, or a fresh vision from God, it comes in the midst of unsettling circumstances that can abort the birthing process. When I was removed from a ministry role years ago, it was tempting to succumb to bitterness. But by the grace of God, I found strength to begin the birthing process of what lay ahead. I chose to rise above the desire for bitterness and focus my energies on birthing something new. This is the snare of the devil that derails many. Many churches proliferate because of divisions or strife. This is not to say that people shouldn't set up churches if they so desire and it is clear that this is what God requires of them. However, many have started churches because they had a disagreement with their pastor or colleague and left in anger and bitterness to start a church. What may seem like a good thing may not be God's idea. The bitterness and pain should drive us to seek God and in so doing give birth to what *He* has in mind.

As a pastor, business person, professional, husband, wife, student, or child, you may find you reach a certain point in your life and everyone around you is proud of your achievements; but somehow your inner man reveals to you that there is more ahead. You can either bask in the adulation of others or seek God's face for direction. Alternatively, you may be coming through a crisis, the loss of a job, a business collapse, or marriage break up. Whatever the circumstances may be, as you seek God, He will bring fresh direction, hope, strength, and even reveal new assignments, new heights to conquer, new territories to infiltrate, or new areas to seek dominion in business. When this happens, you will need to seek the collaboration of the Holy Spirit to incubate and nurture what God has spoken.

At some point, as you stay focused in the place of prayer, you will know when the time of birthing comes. Just as a pregnant woman knows when labor pains come and it is time to give birth, so will you know when labor comes upon you spiritually and it is time to give birth to that child of destiny.

FRUSTRATION

Another way we arrive at a time of birthing is through frustration. In the natural, frustration many times is a reflection of a season of birthing in the spirit. If you find yourself frustrated, resist the temptation to lash out at people around you no matter what the circumstance. The frustration you may be experiencing is an opportunity for great advance and change. So instead of lashing out, pray—for it is a time of rejoicing. If you need to take time off to be alone, do so and channel your energies in the place of prayer. Too many of us are caught up with the everyday issues of life, so God requires shock therapy to get our attention and force us to channel our spiritual energies in the right direction. As you begin, you will be amazed at how a new realm of spiritual reality opens up to you. God begins to align favor, grace, people, revelation, faith, strength, hope, and vigor in you to ensure you give "birth" to what He has ordained.

Never give in to despair except, of course, if it leads you to cry out to God. If it prevents you from crying to God or complaining to God, avoid it like the plague. When you feel despair coming upon you, turn to God and cry to Him. He is always ever so near. God is always ever so close. Do not wallow in self-pity; it is a wasteful and energy dissipating emotion. In a state of despair, we lose sight of God and want to wallow in self-pity. When things are not going well, look inward and enter your birthing chamber. This is the secret to marching on in strength regardless of the circumstances.

My prayer is that as you read, you will receive strength to give birth to destiny. What joy this releases in Heaven when a son or daughter gives birth in due season to his or her God-ordained destiny. The same way we rejoice when a child is born on earth, is the same way the angels rejoice alongside our Father in Heaven when you give birth to your destiny.

WHY AM I HERE?

This charge I commit to you, son Timothy, according to the prophecies previously made concerning you, that by them you may wage the good warfare (1 Timothy 1:18).

Paul's charge to Timothy here is to wage a good warfare because of the prophecies previously made concerning him. Prophecies contain our future. When we receive prophecies, we are not to be laid back and ambivalent concerning those prophecies. Prophecies come to give us direction and provide a roadmap for the present and the future. Prophecies come to ensure that our lives are purposeful and meaningful in the advance of God's glory. Therefore when prophecies are received, it stands to reason that we must ensure that they come to pass.

Having faith and a good conscience, which some having rejected, concerning the faith have suffered shipwreck, of which are Hymenaeus and Alexander, whom I delivered to Satan that they may learn not to blaspheme (1 Timothy 1:19-20).

To wage the good warfare, we must lay the foundation of faith and a good conscience. Without these our warfare would be in vain. Paul goes on to publicly name two men whose lives suffered shipwreck because they did not have faith and a good conscience. It was so bad that he handed them over to satan for them to learn never to blaspheme. What a hard measure he had to adopt. What had Hymenaeus and Alexander rejected? Faith and a good conscience. So faith and a good conscience are essential to ensure that we are not shipwrecked in our relationship with God. Faith is the substance of things hoped and the evidence of things not seen (see Heb. 11:1) and as such, faith substantiates and provides evidence to fuel our hope in whatever prophecy we receive. A good conscience is right standing before God. These are fundamental to waging good warfare concerning whatever has been prophesied. Waging good warfare starts with ensuring that we have the right posture before God.

Too many believers want to run ahead with prophecies they have received but suffer unnecessary shipwreck because they haven't placed a premium on character. There are many gifted pastors, business people, and politicians who received great prophecies but later suffered shipwreck because they did not have faith and a good conscience. So don't be surprised if someone you know was being prepared by God for a great assignment and had received wonderful prophecies only to suffer shipwreck, the reason is that they didn't have the foundation of faith and a good conscience.

Having said that, the next challenge is dealing with the paradox of my human limitation side by side with the fact that I am yet made in the image and likeness of God. While the Bible declares emphatically that I have been made in the image and likeness of God, I know I am still on my journey of being transformed by the renewing of my mind (see Rom. 12:2). In other words, I am a work in progress. So daily I still grapple with all kinds of challenges—including being a good husband and a good father. I strive to do my best to provide for my family. At the same time, while I am passionate about the church's role in advancing the Kingdom of God on earth, I know how slow the process of transformation can be in my life and also in the lives of the men and women who together make up the local assembly where I serve as a resident pastor. I know how often I travail over the life of a brother or sister who is slow in making that much needed transition to overcome character flaws, recurring sin, etc.

This paradox is aptly described in the words of Paul to the Corinthian Christians when he says to them, "But we have this treasure in earthen vessels, that the excellence of the power may be of God and not of us" (2 Cor. 4:7). So many times my life feels like a paradox—an earthen vessel carrying the treasure of God's presence. This earthen vessel of mine is subject to all kinds of challenges. These show up as various fears, insecurities, challenges, disappointments, rejection, pride, greed, lust, etc. The list is endless. Though Christ may dwell in my heart and though I am the seed of Abraham and therefore an heir of the promise, I nevertheless have to grapple with the daily vicissitudes of life.

TRANSFORMATION

Prayer has the power to bridge the vast chasm between the expectation of God's Word and my reality. Prayer can transport me into the atmosphere of God's presence. In God's presence, I am transformed. In God's presence, faith and a good conscience are shaped into my life. Prayer molds me into an accurate vessel to fulfill every prophecy spoken.

For instance, in 1995 I arrived in Denmark as a missionary to pastor a fledgling church that had started meeting a few months before I arrived. Before we arrived, we had received prophecies that we would go into the nations of the world with the gospel of Jesus Christ. When these prophecies came, we were in Lagos worshiping in a local assembly of a well-known denomination. We had no idea how or where we would be going as missionaries or when it would happen. We accepted the prophecies nevertheless. Not only did we accept the prophecies, we waged daily warfare.

Sometimes up to 600 of us would gather to pray. Vigils became commonplace for us. At the time, what we were involved in was unprecedented. It was far more common to hear of European missionaries in Africa and not African missionaries in Europe. Most of us had also never been to Denmark prior to this time. Further still in my case, I had only met a handful of Danes in my life; first in primary school and thereafter during jobs as a student in England in the 1980s. All I knew was that Denmark was a Scandinavian country somewhere in the north of Europe.

So when I arrived in Denmark in June 1995, I was filled with both trepidation and excitement at the privilege of making a difference for the Kingdom of God. However, as excited as I was, it was also a difficult time for me. My fiancé and I had been separated for a few months, and we were finding it difficult to conclude our plans for marriage especially because of my newfound missionary zeal that had taken me to London first and then to Denmark. To make matters worse, my fiancé had been refused a visa to visit me in London, just as I was heading out to Copenhagen. What seemed like a simple refusal, which many Nigerians experience all the time, carried greater significance for us because of the period of separation, wedding plans that were neither here nor there, and of course to my fiancé it seemed that while she was going through the pain of a visa rejection, I was busy, or so it seemed, crisscrossing Europe. My turmoil and the swirl of my emotions can only best be imagined.

A few days after my arrival in Denmark, I was struck down with an illness called shingles. It was strange because apparently I was the wrong race and age for the illness—since the illness typically struck middle-aged Caucasians. As a result of the illness, I was in pain much of the time; I was also listless and fast losing focus and momentum concerning my mission in Denmark. This was my first real missionary foray, and I hadn't even started! Discouragement began to creep in.

In my pain and discomfort, the question I had to settle in my mind was whether Denmark was part of the picture God had ordained or whether it was a misadventure I had embarked upon in my missionary zeal. I cast my mind back to the first time I had watched a video recording of our church's first foray into Denmark and how much I wanted to be part of what I saw. It all seemed suddenly a bit overwhelming as I saw myself helpless and in constant pain thinking *what change could I bring to this country?* But then I began to pray; first for my sanity in the midst of it all.

WAGING WAR

In my discomfort, I began to wage war concerning the prophecies earlier spoken. I knew my being in Denmark was not an accident. This I did by praying in other tongues for extended periods of time. It was uncomfortable, but I persevered as best as I could. As I did, my sense of mission regarding Denmark remained firm and steadfast. I could focus on the task at hand. In my discomfort, I could still focus on the lofty ideals at hand. I discovered an amazing truth that is best reflected in the words of Paul to Timothy:

> *This charge I commit to you, son Timothy, according to the prophecies previously made concerning you, that by them you may wage the good warfare* (1 Timothy 1:18).

I learned that I had to wage war concerning my assignment in Denmark. Finding success in the will of God requires grit and determination that are shaped in the furnace of affliction and difficulties. In these circumstances, you are faced with the reality of whether God called you or not. The only way forward in times like these is to pray. We may be tempted to give up or succumb to the reality of our difficult circumstances, but perseverance is what is what is required. If we succumb to the flesh, the birthing process runs the risk of being aborted, because it requires the push of our spirit in prayer to ensure that in the midst of our affliction, God's purpose is coming forth.

So I persevered in prayer and not only did the pain subside and the sickness come to an end, my fiancé and I went on to marry in Denmark and lead a missionary team there for a year. Our time in Denmark became a time of learning how to intercede for a nation and pierce the veil of darkness with which the devil seeks to blind the eyes of the people. Many people we spoke with said Denmark was the graveyard of missionaries, but we experienced great favor from God, found faithful friends, and could sense the spiritual darkness in the land recede as we persevered in the place of prayer.

A few years later I was at a crossroads in my life. At the time, I was part of a large well-known Nigerian denomination. My senior pastor had just decided to leave to pursue other options in ministry. I wanted to leave also, but it would seem as though I was leaving because of him. What was I to do? I have always written in journals, which help keep track of my walk with God. For me, writing in a journal acts as a way of discerning the will of God. It also helps me clarify the will of God. As I write, it is as though the Holy Spirit directs my thoughts to write what will give me direction. I want to enjoin you to do the same. There are times when I start writing and I know it is just me pouring out my pain. But I have also found that immensely beneficial because at the end of writing I get a clear sense of direction. So in determining what to do about the situation, I started journaling. As I did, I had a clear sense that I had to leave the denomination to embark on a fresh journey. This helped me to move on without worrying about what others would think. I had heard God, and it was truly time to move on.

Our lives in God are pilgrimages, with landscapes we cannot sometimes predict. The joy of the journey is found in our efforts to align ourselves with the heartbeat of our Father.

Chapter 5

Treasure Hunt!

For he who speaks in a tongue does not speak to men but to God, for no one understands him; however, in the spirit he speaks mysteries (1 Corinthians 14:2).

But we speak the wisdom of God in a mystery, the hidden wisdom which God ordained before the ages for our glory, which none of the rulers of this age knew; for had they known, they would not have crucified the Lord of glory (1 Corinthians 2:7-8).

Speaking in diverse tongues is one of the most powerful gifts of the Holy Spirit. The first time I spoke in tongues I was amazed at what happened to me because at the time I didn't believe in it! I couldn't understand how I would make what seemed like unintelligible sounds and that would qualify as speaking to God. When it happened, I was praying for someone who was going to have his leg amputated. I desperately didn't want the amputation to take place because the man I was praying for was soon to be married to a secretary in my office. I just couldn't imagine the man on crutches walking down the aisle. As I prayed desperately in English, at some point I ran out of things to say and next thing I knew I was saying things that were unintelligible to me. Thus began my journey into this new realm of prayer.

Like Paul, my boast very often is that I thank God I speak in tongues more than you all (see 1 Cor. 14:18). All of eternity will not be sufficient to discover all the benefits and power of speaking in tongues. Only eternity will reveal all the things we have averted just by speaking in tongues. In the same way, only time will tell the grace imparted into our lives to discover and do the will of God as we prayed in tongues. Who will know how many lives were transformed because somebody somewhere was praying in tongues? Praying in tongues is God's great secret weapon for confounding the wisdom of the wise and routing every conspiracy of the devil.

Praying in Tongues

For many years now, I have established the discipline of praying in tongues for an hour or two every day. On some days, I pray for three hours. The transformation in my life can only best be experienced for it to be understood. When I pray in tongues consistently, I discover I am far more efficient than I imagined possible. I am far less likely to be distracted by unnecessary time-wasting activity. I am better at spotting and averting problems before they arise.

> For he who speaks in a tongue does not speak to men but to God, ...in the spirit he speaks mysteries (1 Corinthians 14:2).

Over the years, I have come to treasure the gift of speaking in tongues for many reasons. In this chapter, though, I want to focus on one prophetic benefit of speaking in tongues. Paul's first epistle to the Corinthians is very instructive. "For he who speaks in a tongue does not speak to men but to God, ...in the spirit he speaks mysteries." I have often asked myself what God had in mind when He gave this revelation to Paul the apostle.

The first question that comes to mind is, "What mysteries are being spoken?" Clearly it is one thing to talk about the mysteries of God but it is yet another to talk about the mysteries of God which we speak! However, when we read this verse in conjunction with First Corinthians 2:7-13, it opens up a new realm of revelation.

> *But we speak the wisdom of God in a mystery, the hidden wisdom which God ordained before the ages for our glory, which none of the rulers of this age knew; for had they known, they would not have crucified the Lord of glory. But as it is written: "Eye has not seen, nor ear heard, nor have entered into the heart of man the things which God has prepared for those who love Him." But God has revealed them to us through His Spirit. For the Spirit searches all things, yes, the deep things of God. For what man knows the things of a man except the spirit of the man which is in him? Even so no one knows the things of God except the Spirit of God. Now we have received, not the spirit of the world, but the Spirit who is from God, that we might know the things that have been freely given to us by God. These things we also speak, not in words which man's wisdom teaches but which the Holy Spirit teaches, comparing spiritual things with spiritual (1 Corinthians 2:7-13).*

From verses 1 to 6 of chapter 2, Paul had been expounding on the difference between the wisdom of men and the wisdom of God. Then in verse 7 he declares, "But we speak the wisdom of God in a mystery, the hidden wisdom which God ordained before the ages for our glory." When read in the context of the previous verses, Paul is clearly making reference to Jesus Christ. However from a prophetic perspective, we can see something more. We can apply fresh insight to this revelation when we read it in conjunction with First Corinthians 14:2. Both Scriptures refer to speaking and to speaking mysteries.

In addition though, First Corinthians 2:7 speaks of mysteries as the hidden wisdom of God, ordained from before the ages for our glory. Read together, a new dimension of prayer opens up. We can then say that he who speaks in a new tongue does not speak to men, but to God; and in the realm of the spirit, he speaks mysteries—the hidden wisdom of God, ordained from before the ages for our glory. So when I speak in tongues, I am bringing back to God His hidden wisdom, spoken in a mystery, which He had ordained from before the ages for my glory. When I speak in tongues, I open up the vast treasure house of what God ordained before the ages for my glory! What an awesome gateway to destiny that praying in tongues then provides.

When I pray in tongues, it goes beyond the need to be edified and all the other benefits that praying in tongues provides. By praying in tongues, I begin the process of uncovering purpose, which in my natural self I am unable to discern let alone pray about. As I pray, the Spirit of God who searches all things and even the deep things of God brings revelation to my heart. As I pray, I uncover purpose buried deep in the heart of God. My praying becomes a tool for bringing my life into alignment with what God had ordained thousands of years before.

Praying in tongues becomes a supernatural gateway that converts me into a miner as I drill deep into the heart of God. I believe one of the fundamental reasons for praying this way is that when we pray in our own understanding, we are limited by the fact that in our human wisdom, except by occasional revelation from God, we cannot search deep into the heart of God and receive understanding. However when we pray in tongues, we are not speaking to others but to God; and therefore our speaking brings our spirits into a new dimension with God. This dimension allows the Spirit of God to probe deep into the heart of God to uncover what God has ordained.

SPEAKING TO GOD

One of the best ways to understand this process is when we liken it to what happens when we search a computer for lost files or folders. When we type a word as a clue, a lamp icon appears and begins to search all the drives in the computer. This process is normally exhaustive as the search is through every file and folder. In the same fashion, when we pray in tongues, the Spirit of God "searches all things, yes, the deep things of God" (1 Cor. 2:10).

Further, this kind of praying bypasses human understanding "for he who speaks in a tongue does not speak to men" (1 Cor. 14:2). It also confounds demonic powers "which none of the rulers of this age knew; for had they known, they would not have crucified the Lord of glory" (1 Cor. 2:8). What an awesome gift!

There are many key pointers to what God has in mind from this Scripture. God is a Spirit and worship of God must be in spirit and truth. In other words, God operates in a spiritual realm or context and it is imperative that as children of God we relate to God in the same realm. The challenge, though, is that unlike God who is Spirit, we are spirit, soul, and body. Therefore our relationship with God is dependent on being spiritual. It is not based on our feelings or intellect or whether we are hungry, tired, or ill. Nevertheless, God's tender, loving, and compassionate nature understands the challenges we face as we rise above our flesh and our souls to relate with Him spiritually. The gift of speaking in other tongues becomes the supernatural gateway to God. It bypasses our intellect, emotions, feelings, and flesh in order for us to receive from the heart of God. The power of this gift rests in God providing a fast track route to Him through speaking in tongues.

When we speak in tongues, we exercise a channel of communication that is exclusively unto God. Except someone has the gift of interpretation, what we speak to God is exclusively for God. That is why the Scripture says "for no one understands him; however, in the spirit he speaks mysteries" (1 Cor. 14:2). Our minds are unfruitful too! Except, of course, we have the gift of interpretation. This gift allows us to communicate in a language that accurately communicates what should critically be flowing unto God. It therefore bypasses our feelings, emotions, or flesh. We are less prone to pray the way we feel because speaking in tongues transforms the language of communication to God. It ensures I speak what God needs to hear or what God desires to hear. It is not that God is unmindful of my feelings or emotions. God is a tender loving Father full of "loving kindness and tender mercies" (Ps. 103:4).

Rather, it shows us a dimension of prayer where we come to God based on what He has in mind, and we take advantage of this gift as a tool that guarantees that God gets what He wants. What a great privilege to have a language for exclusive communication to God! All of eternity would not be sufficient to know all the mysteries that are spoken when we speak in tongues. However, we can gain some insight into what these mysteries represent.

Hidden Wisdom of God

When we pause and reflect for a moment, we discover an awesome truth, which is that the mysteries we speak are the hidden wisdom of God. You might ask, Why are they hidden? The truth is nothing great is found on the highways and byways of life. Jesus told a parable of the Kingdom of God and described the Kingdom of God as a treasure buried in a field which, when found, the person who found it went and bought the whole field. The point is, the Kingdom was compared to a buried treasure. The best things are to be sought out. That is why the prophet Amos exclaimed, "Surely the Lord God does nothing, unless He reveals His secret to his servants the prophets" (Amos 3:7).

Speaking in tongues becomes like a treasure hunt. When we speak, we are drilling deep into the heart of God speaking the wisdom of God, which had been hidden in a mystery. As we speak, we uncover what God had ordained or planned from before the ages—from the dateless past for our glory. Glory is the ultimate objective! By speaking in tongues, we can walk in the glory of God.

God has an inexhaustible treasure regarding our destiny; His favor, grace, assignments, marriage, children, and whatever else can be imagined, are ordained for a preappointed time. God desires that we richly enjoy all He has in store for us. To us all these things are mysteries because we cannot decipher when and where they will happen. However, when we pray in tongues we reach deep into the treasure of God. To the unspiritual, all these things are unintelligible. To receive and benefit from something that is a mystery requires a language that can decode the things in the heart of God. It requires comparing spiritual with spiritual (see 1 Cor. 2:13). If God were to attempt to communicate to us some measure of His plans and purposes and the intricate working out of those plans and purposes, it would be impossible for us to grasp this knowledge in its variety, timing, and manner of execution. What is necessary is the gift of speaking in diverse kinds of tongues, which then becomes a channel of communication for the Holy Spirit to download into our spirits the plans and purposes of God. When they are downloaded into our spirits, over time the Spirit of God causes illumination, understanding, and prophetic insight to come to us such that we respond accurately to what is already in our spirits through the speaking of tongues.

SPEAKING MYSTERIES

As mentioned previously, in August 2008, a friend and I started a daily prayer project. We decided to commit two hours of our time every morning to speak mysteries unto God. It is now well over one year since we started. Most times when we have met to pray, our focus has been simply that: speaking mysteries unto God. We see ourselves as tools in God's hands to be used to establish His will. This revelation has allowed us to pray sometimes for hours nonstop. Many times as we pray we can sense our vocabulary change. Other times we sense an increase in intensity. Its like and ebb and flow as we exercise this wonderful gift.

The changes we have experienced have been monumental. I am more sensitive to the will of God. For instance, in 2007 and 2008, I was in turmoil many times trying to balance the time I was spending as a founding partner in a law practice and the time I was spending as the resident pastor in my local assembly. Many times I felt as though I was being torn in two. My senior pastor felt I wasn't doing enough as a resident pastor, while my partners in the law firm felt they had lost me to the church. To make matters worse, since my partners were Christians they didn't want to sound as though they were unmindful of this other life especially as it had to do with the church.

Sometimes I wondered if I should abandon the law firm and focus on the church solely. Other times I wondered if I should focus on law alone. The more I prayed, the clearer it became. I wasn't to do either. I realized God was sharpening my focus on the areas of my life where He sought fruit—such as writing and teaching. So I rearranged my affairs accordingly. I moved from being an equity partner in my law firm to an "of counsel" role. This freed up equity for me and freed my partners from paying me an allowance. I could now focus on writing and teaching.

I hadn't realized that this was the plan in God's heart for me until I prayed in tongues to dredge deep into the heart of God and uncover what He had ordained from the dateless past for this appointed time. This book is a product of the time I have freed up to ensure I exercise this gift of writing. I am 47 years of age and many would consider the kind of move I have made reckless, especially as my wife and I have 4 children aged between 2 and 12 years. However, the confidence to do what God desires only comes as we uncover the hidden wisdom of God.

Another challenge we are overcoming, as we have stayed steadfast in this kind of praying, has been the challenge of raising a new cadre of leaders for our ministry. In 2006 our ministry started an intensive missions initiative to the slum dwellings in the city of Lagos. To spearhead this move, our senior pastor and a team of approximately 100 pastors and leaders set up a base in the center of the city and rescue mission outposts in over 20 different locations. This singular move stripped our home church of 90 percent of its mature and seasoned leaders. It took the past two to three years of grueling hard work for us to begin to reproduce a new cadre of leaders. Had we not been praying, there were many times we would have been blown away by the winds of adversity, offense, and spiritual burn-out. However, after three years into the project, we are stronger, more mature, and even more hungry for what God has in store for us.

I challenge you to embark upon this treasure hunt. Though God's ways are too vast and unsearchable to ever fully understand, we can hope to tap into a measure of His glory, power, wisdom, favor, life, grace, love, joy, peace, understanding, destiny, and whatever else you can imagine. Start with a time of day that suits you. Give yourself one hour. This may seem impossible to you. It is not. Do not underestimate the power of God in You. Happy treasure hunting!

CHAPTER 6

Thy Kingdom Come

UNITING HEAVEN AND EARTH

Now it came to pass, as He was praying in a certain place, when He ceased, that one of His disciples said to Him, "Lord teach us to pray, as John also taught his disciples." So He said to them, "When you pray, say: Our Father in heaven, hallowed be Your name. Your kingdom come. Your will be done on earth as it is in heaven" (Luke 11:1-2).

The day I was able to make a connection with this Scripture in Luke and the expectation that God has that I will exercise dominion on the earth, it changed my life forever. It opened up a completely new dimension to prayer that I never saw before. It was like clicking on an icon on your computer and discovering a new world you never knew actually existed.

Exercising dominion on earth requires unlocking certain doors in the spiritual realm. When this happens, a vast new world of endless possibilities opens up before us. When Jesus taught the disciples to pray "Your kingdom come. Your will be done on earth as it is in heaven," He was introducing them to the power God has made available to introduce Heaven on earth. Heaven on earth is the beginning of our dominion. God's Kingdom in Heaven is undisputed. But on earth it was lost to the devil and has now been restored by Jesus. In Heaven, God's will was never in dispute; however, on earth it was disputed by the devil because Adam lost dominion. But again Jesus has restored it. Nonetheless, in teaching the disciples to pray, Jesus declared that they should pray, "Your kingdom come. Your will be done on earth as it is in heaven." But why would Jesus ask them to pray for something He was set to recover from the devil on the cross? Was this not an irrelevant thing to do? Is this prayer still relevant today?

The prayer is as relevant and critical today as it was in Jesus' day. Though Jesus recovered the legal mandate to have dominion on earth, this prayer provides the infiltration and enforcement of this mandate by each one of us in our sphere of influence. In the mid-1990s, I was part of a missionary effort to plant churches in different parts of Europe, especially in countries considered very resistant to the gospel of Jesus Christ. When I arrived in Denmark, I was greatly inspired by the fact that I was God's co-laborer whose assignment was to usher in the Kingdom of God into that nation. The words of Jesus in Luke 11:1-2 suddenly resonated with powerful new insight.

On a typical Sunday, our church would have approximately 20 adults in attendance. Many of them were immigrants and asylum seekers of West African and East African origin. This really troubled me because my passion in coming to Denmark was to reach the native Danes. Incredibly as we prayed these Scriptures, we began to make contact with many Danes outside of planned church meetings. I even cultivated a close friendship with a particular gentleman who later became my prayer partner, and together we spent hours praying and ushering the full dimension of God's reign over the fabric of the entire nation. I believe what happened was our praying introduced a dimension of God's grace that transcended cultural barriers. It made a reality of the fact that in God's Kingdom there is neither male or female, Gentile or Jew but rather all can become one in Christ (see Gal. 3:28).

DECLARING AND DECREEING

Praying also made us very bold because we now had revelation and insight, and we could see the fruit of praying in this manner. Previously when the alien nature of Danish culture would have limited us, we had a new boldness because we were declaring and decreeing something better and superior—even to the Danes who could claim such an illustrious history as the descendants of Vikings and one of the direct beneficiaries of Martin Luther's reformation.

Armed with this prayer strategy, many colleagues of mine moved into other nations including the United Kingdom, Germany, Haiti, and Jamaica. At the time, our strategy globally was to set up churches to operate on two tiers. Some we called centers or governing bases because of their strategic locations in capital cities with regional relevance beyond their national boundaries such as the churches we planted in London and Washington, DC. Others we called frontline missions because they were to spearhead the thrust into surrounding nations. This two-tier strategy was in essence no different from the strategy adopted by the apostles in the Book of Acts. In their case, they set out from Jerusalem and established bases in Antioch and Ephesus and frontline missions spearheading a further thrust into the surrounding regions through the work they did in Philippi, Thessalonica, Berea, Corinth, etc.

Each time I reflect on this strategy, I can't help exclaiming like Paul, "Oh, the depths of the riches both of the wisdom and knowledge of God! How unsearchable are His judgments and His ways past finding out!" (See Romans 11:33.) Isn't it amazing, that though God is sovereign, yet He desires our collaboration to bring His will to pass? In other words, each time I pray in this fashion my prayer has the power to change circumstances! Not only that, it has the power to enthrone something else entirely. This revelation is fundamental to prayer. It underscores our primary role on earth as children of God. Since we are citizens of Heaven, our presence on earth is to bring Heaven to earth. We are the conduits through which the atmosphere of Heaven is introduced on earth. This is what the devil hates and resists with all his power.

In Denmark we prayed for hours and many of the pastors of other churches were amazed that we spent that amount of time praying. Did we need to spend that amount of time praying? Surely God had heard! But we knew that to displace the devil and his cohorts in a region and introduce the atmosphere, culture, values, and liberty of the Kingdom of God would take hours of fervent praying—our prayers were dismantling demonic strongholds and building new Kingdom patterns in the spirit realm. This had to be done first before its manifestation in our lives.

There is much ground to cover especially in recovering revelation about the purpose of prayer. As I said earlier, the principle behind Jesus' teaching on prayer is traceable to man's original purpose—dominion. When our forebears, Adam and Eve, sinned, they lost fellowship with God and dominion over God's creation. When Jesus died on the cross, He restored fellowship with God and dominion over God's creation. However, to walk in fellowship with God and exercise dominion on earth, we must have faith in God and revelation of the full import of Jesus' victory at the cross. In the posture of prayer, the words "your kingdom come" and "your will be done on earth as it is in heaven" are like decrees and declarations reestablishing our right to exercise dominion on earth.

SHIFT IN THINKING

In these words of Jesus we also learn that prayer is primarily about what God desires to see expressed on earth. This revelation can be quite difficult to stomach especially as it is common practice among Christians to think that prayer is essentially for us to make our petitions and supplications to God. No doubt we should make our petitions to God, but we must recognize that prayer is essentially about what God desires. The reality is that Jesus taught that we are agents of God commanded to beseech Him to bring Heaven to earth. This realization brings about a complete shift in thinking. Many opportunities to shape the world or make it conducive for us to have dominion in all spheres—whether in the marketplace, media, education, or politics—are lost because no one stands in the gap to pray as our Father in Heaven desires.

As a lawyer, I have also seen the benefit of this kind of praying. In Nigeria, there are certain challenges we face in the marketplace. As mentioned previously, certain corrupt practices have become accepted as the way of doing business. There are many organizations that only do business after being offered some kind of financial inducement. Worse yet, many Christians request and offer these bribes too! So we are faced with a scenario similar to that in the days of the Judges when the children of Israel did as they pleased, after the death of Joshua and all the elders who outlived Joshua, who had seen all the great works of the Lord.

Prophetically speaking, therefore, this kind of praying reestablishes the ancient landmarks of God's sovereignty and will over the affairs of our communities. In my law firm, we quickly recognized that our role was not simply one of being good, ethical lawyers or ambassadors of the Kingdom of God but in addition we saw a role defined for us as intercessors decreeing that the Kingdom of God come on earth in our profession, as it is Heaven. This was particularly exciting for us because our legal training gave us particular insight into the power of a decree especially with our recent history of military dictatorships when a decree from the military ruler was immediately enforced without delay of any sort!

It made me also wonder how, tragically, many sectors of human activity are in darkness because God can't find willing collaborators who will usher in the Kingdom of God. I pray you will stand for God as an intercessor in your profession or place of influence in the marketplace. Brett Johnson, who runs a marketplace ministry called The Institute for Innovation, Integration, and Impact, estimates that because of globalization the marketplace globally has the largest homogenous people group to reach. This means many of us in the marketplace can, through our jobs, professions, and entrepreneurial activities, extend the frontiers of the Kingdom through strategic intercession like never before.

OPEN THE GATES

When this becomes our prayer stance, it opens up a whole new vista of spiritual activity and power. It changes our vocabulary as the words we speak resonate with the revelation of the assignment at hand. It opens up previously unseen treasures in His Word. David was one man who understood this fact well as can be read throughout the Psalms. In Psalm 110:2, David states, "The Lord shall send the rod of Your strength out of Zion. Rule in the midst of your enemies!" In other words, out of the church (Zion), the authority (rod) of God's strength is extended for rulership even in a time when demonic hosts (our enemies) are all around us. With a promise like this, we speak with authority and boldness declaring that we are the rod of God's strength from the place of His habitation—Zion. When these words are spoken, the spirit realm responds to swiftly accord with God's dominion because it agrees with the protocol of the Kingdom of God. The enemies of God are set in disarray because someone with understanding speaks words that are designed for a specific kind of impact in the spirit realm. With this kind of prayer, angelic hosts are purposefully summoned to execute righteous judgment.

On another occasion, David, in Psalm 24, declares that the earth is the Lord's and the fullness thereof and goes on to describe a generation who are like Jacob because they are seekers of God who will command gates restricting access to open up to the Kingdom of God. The gates referred to in this Scripture are not physical gates. The spirit realm functions very much the same way as the physical realm. This Scripture provides illumination on how to lift barriers and usher in the Kingdom of God in power and dominion.

This type of prayer opens up limitless opportunities because it has the power to unlock all kinds of demonic structures. It can break down strongholds of culture, religion, and race because it involves a wholesale shift of demonic positions and an ushering in of the Kingdom of God. With this type of prayer, entire regions, business sectors, and family strongholds are blown away. When the big picture is set in place and there is overarching dominion of the Kingdom of God, the day-to-day challenges of living the sanctified life and dealing with demonic activity are dealt with routinely.

As a pastor, many times I have had the privilege of counseling with people going through challenging circumstances including marriage, children on drugs, financial ruin, and death. On many occasions, the circumstances have looked bleak and hopeless. But even in the bleakest circumstance, for instance when a marriage is about to break up, the minute revelation of God's will transcends into the equation and everything begins to change. What is even more amazing is watching the transforming power of prayer overcome pain and bitterness. Collaborating with God without a doubt unleashes a dimension of grace and power that is limitless.

Some may think you need to be "super spiritual" to collaborate with God like this. But this is far from the truth. God delights in our weakness and inability. The truth is that our weakness and inability are the exact qualities that qualify us to collaborate with God. This is what confounds the kingdom of darkness. When we acknowledge our weakness and consequently our desperate need for God, we become perfect candidates for the strength of God to be perfected in us.

Let us together extend the frontiers of God's rule in our lives, our families, our communities, and the nations of the world by collaborating fervently and passionately with God to see His Kingdom stretch across all kinds of frontiers worldwide.

DARE TO BE DIFFERENT

By faith Enoch was taken away so that he did not see death, and was not found, because God had taken him; for before he was taken he had this testimony, that he pleased God (Hebrews 11:5).

The Book of Jude records that Enoch was born seven generations from Adam. Genesis records that 65 years after Enoch was born he fathered Methuselah. Genesis also records that after Methuselah was born Enoch began walking with God and walked with Him for the next 300 years after which Enoch disappeared, because God had taken him. In the 300 years in which he walked with God, Enoch had other sons and daughters but nevertheless one day he disappeared. Now of everyone born prior to Enoch there is no record of anyone who stood out and was identified as a man who walked with God. The record of the men born prior to Enoch simply says they lived for a certain number of years and thereafter they died. So in his day, Enoch stood out for two reasons: he was known to have walked with God, and he was translated and therefore never experienced death. From the Book of Jude we also discover that Enoch prophesied about the coming judgment of God.

In Enoch's day, men lived very long and so Enoch's first son, Methuselah, is recorded as having lived the longest dying at the age of 969 years. Adam also lived very long and died at the age of 930 years. So these men had long years of interaction with each other. Now after Seth's son, Enosh, was born, men began to call upon God. Perhaps the tragedy of the first recorded murder was so shocking (Cain killing Abel, see Gen. 4:8) that after Seth's child, Enosh, was born men began to sense the need to reconnect with God and began calling upon Him. Or perhaps they heard Adam describe the closeness he once had with God in the Garden of Eden and how God would come down in the cool of the evening and talk with Adam. It is not clear what the catalyst was, but men began to call on God!

Another interesting feature about the times in which they lived was since Enoch was seven generations from Adam, it meant Adam was alive and would have been 622 years old at the time Enoch was born. For the 300-year period during which Enoch walked with God, Adam was around for the first 243 years, as he lived for 930 years. While no one can say for certain if Adam and Enoch ever interacted, there is a strong likelihood they did. I suspect that Enoch would have at least sought out Adam because Adam was the first man on earth! Surely having an illustrious figure like Adam around would fill a person with curiosity about how it all started with God. I would, given the same opportunity!

Because Enoch had the unique distinction of walking with God, the questions that agitate my mind are, *What did it mean to have walked with God? What was the nature of the relationship he had with God? Why did he alone have this distinction? What was he yearning for that others before couldn't find or didn't search for? How did he know he had connected with God? What insights did he receive from God to cause him to prophesy about the impending judgment of God?*

My guess is that Enoch would have heard and probably spoken with Adam about the momentous events that led to Adam's expulsion from the Garden and separation from God. He would also have heard of the tragic death of Abel and the comfort Adam's family had with the arrival of baby Seth whose name simply meant God has given me another one. Enoch probably would have met the men who were talking of reaching out to God and possibly joined on a few occasions as they called on God with a hunger and passion to experience fellowship with the God of the heavens and the earth.

In all this, what probably stood out most in Enoch's mind would have been what he lost. Possibly he knew there could be more than just calling out to God. Possibly he knew that if we really do hunger for God, He reaches down and picks us up. It may have started with calling on God with a passionate heart cry until he could feel the palpable presence of God. He possibly persevered egged on by the thinking that if God desired fellowship with Adam, He would also want it with him. Enoch probably persevered until he broke free from the seeming inevitability of his day.

There are three places in the Bible where Enoch is mentioned. The first is in Genesis where the account of Enoch's life, in a short paragraph, captures something unprecedented, something unimaginable, a shining meteor in a day of gross darkness on the earth. Who can fathom the depths of the riches of the ways of God! Who can fathom the pathways of greatness that await the man or woman who yearns for the living God! Enoch's second mention is in the great hall of faith in Hebrews chapter 11. By faith he pleased God and because he pleased God, he was taken away by God. For all eternity, one man's singular passion introduced unprecedented events on the earth. Third, Enoch is mentioned in the Book of Jude as a man prophesying in his day of the impending judgment of God upon men who had perverted the way of God. What a man, what a legacy!

ENOCH'S EXAMPLE

Enoch's life is an example of living above the low standards of sin and the prevailing standards of men. It was Enoch's hunger for deep fellowship with God that introduced him to an unimaginable dimension of life. We need to be hungry for something unprecedented in our day. We must desire to be blazing lights in our generation and to achieve what we need to be like Enoch—transcending the prevailing standards of our day. We need to channel our energies into seeking God such that we become witnesses to our generation. This dimension of grace is expressed as "walking with God." It is the place of divine constraints, promptings, and leading where we cannot afford to be out of step.

We live in perilous times when the love of God is declining. Today many are ready to break God's laws if they appear inconvenient. I know women who are so desperate to marry that they would marry men who don't share their core values about God just to have the tag "married." I know men who, when the chips are down, will cheat and lie to gain some financial advantage. Today many in the church can no longer counsel against divorce because like a Trojan horse divorce is now commonplace even among the leadership of our churches. These are the times in which we live; and therefore, like Enoch, we must buck the trend of our day in order to be the shining lights of our generation.

The question is, How does this translate to prayer? What must we discover in the 21st century that Enoch discovered? We read in Hebrews chapter 11:5-6:

> By faith Enoch was taken away so that he did not see death, and was not found, because God had taken him; for before he was taken he had this testimony, that he pleased God. But without faith it is impossible to please Him, for he who comes to God must believe that He is, and that He is a rewarder of those who diligently seek Him.

I am inspired by two things about the life of Enoch. First is the fact that he bucked the trend. He wholeheartedly sought to please God.

Enoch's desire was very simple. He just wanted to make God happy. For Enoch it wasn't the exposition of a great vision or some great sacrifice, it was the fact that he pleased God. This was Enoch's legacy. This single fact brought him into the hall of fame in the Book of Hebrews. So one of the great clouds of witnesses who urge us on as we strive to make our mark in our day is Enoch who pleased God!

In addition, we find that Enoch pleased God because he diligently pursued God! Without a doubt there are many ways in which our diligent pursuit of God can be measured. Whatever they maybe, the chief expression of our diligent pursuit of God will be expressed in prayer. Prayer is the chief outlet of our yearning for God. It is in the place of our supplication that our pursuit for God is expressed. Our deepest yearnings and hunger can only be satisfied as we embrace the closet of prayer. It is in prayer that our hearts resonate with the words of the psalmist in Psalm 42:1-2:

> *As the deer pants for the water brooks, so pants my soul for You, O God. My soul thirsts for God, for the living God. When shall I come and appear before God?*

Prayer must become the deepest expression of our longing for God. It is this kind of yearning that shapes the words we bring and cause us to walk with God. Our generation must produce men and women with the DNA of Enoch.

Shall we in our day experience a physical translation the way Enoch did? Probably, but more than that there is a quality of relationship that we can be translated to experience for those whose hearts pant after God. These are the children of God all of creation is groaning in expectation to see. These men and women will exhibit a quality of life that can only be described as the weightiness of the glory of God. Paul captured the essence of this life when he wrote to the church in Rome saying, "For as many as are led by the spirit of God, these are the sons of God" (Rom. 8:14).

CULTURE OF PRAYER

You might wonder *Why should we hunger for this intangible dimension of life? How would that deal with my everyday challenges?* These are valid questions. However, Christianity was never only about our welfare. Beyond our well-being is the fact that Christianity is ultimately about the glory of Christ being revealed in the church. We cannot afford to lose sight of this goal.

When some friends and I determined to pray every day, sometimes we ask ourselves whether this sacrifice is worth it. It's easier sometimes to focus on some tangible objectives as we pray. However, when we think of Enoch shining like a star for 300 years and whose only distinction was that he walked with God, we are encouraged to seek the glory of God in our day. Once again the words of the Psalm 42:7-8 ring out clearly:

> *Deep calls unto deep at the noise of Your waterfalls; all Your waves and billows have gone over me. The Lord will command His lovingkindness in the daytime, and in the night His song shall be with me—a prayer to the God of my life.*

As a pastor, this is the culture of prayer I seek to establish in the lives of my friends. This approach to prayer introduces an apostolic culture to the church so that all and sundry in church will never lose sight of the goal the glory of God manifest in its fullness in the church. To put it in the words of Paul, "Christ in me the hope of glory" (see Col. 1:27).

However, it is tough because the apostolic culture can sometimes come across as being insensitive to our human frailties and weaknesses. Many in our churches are hurting from all kinds of pains and a call to seek the glory of God may seem too far removed from what they face every day.

I am keenly aware of this living in the city of Lagos. Nevertheless, we don't have a choice but to establish this culture. Ultimately built into this apostolic culture is the strength to overcome all odds. Recently I have been part of a rescue mission into the worst slums in Lagos. Conditions in these slums are so bad it is a miracle to find people living and making a living there. As we venture into these slums, we meet hardened criminals, murderers, prostitutes, child sex slaves, drug addicts, drug dealers, etc.

We go as deliverers with the message of hope, and we take provisions and a medical team to attend to the desperate needs we encounter. For those who are willing to follow us, we begin a discipleship program alongside attempts to empower. The focus of our discipleship is to quickly immerse them in a passionate hunger for God expressed in prayer. Anything less leaves them prone to the lure of the life they are escaping. The answer is an intense boot camp program in which we seek to "birth" revelation and hunger for God. The amazing miracle is the transforming power of prayer as former prostitutes and drug addicts begin to express hunger for God, as something in the spirit realm is unlocked in their favor.

Oh how the heart of God yearns for the Enochs of our day. My prayer is that we will refuse to settle for less in our pursuit of God. The challenge we must overcome is the lie of the devil that makes us feel the glory of God is something abstract with little benefit for the challenges of the every day. This is not so. Glory is deeply embedded in the expectation of God. Enoch's shining example must be our inspiration.

CHAPTER 7

Project Praying

*Now it came to pass in those days that He went out to the mountain to **pray**, and **He continued all night in prayer** to God. And when it was day, He called His disciples to Himself; and from them He chose twelve whom He also named apostles (Luke 6:12).*

This verse in Luke shows that prayer must precede every important or great decision. Jesus is our best example in this regard. He understood the critical importance of praying before important decisions were made. He had determined He was going to select 12 out of all the disciples who followed Him, whom He would appoint as apostles. This was probably the most important decision Jesus had to make concerning the future of His ministry on earth. These apostles were going to go through all kinds of trials and persecutions. They would lay the foundation of the apostolic culture of the early church. They would be responsible for extending the frontiers of the church beyond its Jewish origins.

To illustrate this point clearly, I discovered on a trip to Ukraine that Andrew the apostle had visited the land now known as Ukraine. Imagine the distance he covered to achieve this feat at the time, probably traveling months or years before arriving at Ukraine. This shows very clearly the global impact that Jesus had in mind when He set some aside to become apostles.

Not only that, but Jesus was faced with the challenge of succession. He had come to earth on a mission of salvation, reconciliation, and the restoration of humankind to the original state of glory that God intended. He knew His assignment was intended to last for all generations. Jesus lived on earth with a deep sense of the enormity of His assignment on earth. As the firstborn among many brethren to be, He could not afford to have apostles who would buckle under the first sign of pressure. He needed men who would be faithful to the Truth. He needed men who would pay any price for the advance of the Kingdom of God.

Jesus had to ensure that those who would come after Him would do greater works than He had done. Jesus was determined that His ministry would not be a one-person, superstar ministry but rather one that would keep growing in strength, vigor, and relevance even though He would no longer be present physically. This was more than leaving a legacy; this was about the future of humankind!

Jesus Prayed

Nevertheless, so many questions go through my mind as to why Jesus would pray at all, let alone spend all night praying before choosing those who would be apostles from among the disciples. It is one thing to pray, but why spend a whole night praying? What kept Him going on throughout the night? What issues did He bring before God? What challenges did He need to surmount? Was it a question of who He would choose? Was He praying about their destinies? Was He wrestling in advance with principalities and powers about the wiles the devil would bring before the apostles? How did He pray? Did He speak in other tongues?

Whatever the issues and whatever the manner of His praying, the fact remains that Jesus spent all night calling upon God. Beyond all these questions, I have often wondered, *Why did Jesus, of all people, exemplify prayer? What did Jesus pray about that He didn't know already?*

When I connect Jesus' prayer with the later successes of the apostles, I see a powerful principle at work. Peter, despite his initial denial, would go on to be the catalyst for the first church in Jerusalem. He would also write two epistles. James would become a major stabilizing force in the early church, effectively resolving the thorny issue of circumcision for non-Jews. John the beloved would write many books of the Bible including the Book of Revelation while on the island of Patmos. Not to mention Matthew, Mark, Luke, John, and a host of others.

Many things inspire me about Jesus' example. First is His appetite to pray. He clearly did not approach prayer as a ritual. Too many of us approach prayer the way we brush our teeth or shower in the morning. Prayer has become like a necessary ritual. I watch my wife many times in the morning as she checks whether our children are ready for school. Without fail, I hear questions such as, "Have you brushed your teeth?" "Have you combed your hair?" She is ensuring that our children are ready to face the world.

Unfortunately, this is how many of us perceive prayer. When our praying becomes ritualistic and devoid of the joy of interaction with God, then something is not quite right. Prayer was always intended to be a deep overflowing wellspring of life from which we drink of the immeasurable grace, power, life, wisdom, and direction of God. This is why Jesus would spend all night praying and come away certain of the type of decision He needed to make.

A SPIRITUALLY NOURISHED LIFE

Without a doubt, anyone seeking to break from the ritual of perfunctory prayer will have to contend with major lifestyle changes. This is our big challenge in the 21st century. Many times I have been tempted to think that Jesus could do what He did because He didn't have to contend with big city issues such as traffic or long hours commuting, grueling working hours, a hectic social life, and the demands of technology like the now ubiquitous mobile email and Internet devices from which there is no hiding place. The real challenge I believe is choosing between a spiritually famished life and a spiritually nourished life. Too often we struggle with issues we have no business struggling with, all because we have not nourished our spirits in the wellsprings of God's presence.

As a pastor, I meet many people who are spiritually malnourished seeking a breakthrough from God. This poverty of spirit can only be addressed by the abundance of God's spiritual provision. Many of us have been seduced by a lie of the devil that success is a result of toil and labor. To a large degree this is, of course, true. But everything we deal with in the natural must first have been addressed in the spiritual realm. Our success is based first on ensuring that we align things in the natural to agree with the spiritual realm. I wonder many times about the many challenges in business, marriage, children, career choices, politics, etc., which could have been averted if we had drunk deeply from the wellsprings of God's presence. Too often we forget that friendship with the world is enmity with God.

That is not to say that we should not interact with people; but rather when we do, we don't compromise our values. Our adversary the devil is vicious and is committed to a lifelong fight to the death. We must never underestimate the contrary nature of the world. The ways of God are in complete opposition to the value system of the world. To succeed as a God-centered, Kingdom-minded entrepreneur, for instance, you have to build into your business an apostolic culture.

Some features of this culture go beyond godly values in business relationships and employee welfare. Some of these values involve praying God-given ideas for dominance in a way that reveals the glory of God. Too many Christians are content with a testimony of godly values in their personal lives but don't see that this is just the first step.

Beyond my life is the advance of God's Kingdom in the sphere of influence God has given me. An apostolic culture seeks to express much more. It seeks to express the power and preeminence of God's Kingdom. So a Kingdom-minded businessperson who understands the need to enthrone an apostolic culture knows that it is critical that his or her business has strength, longevity, and the ability to stand out not only in ethics but also as a center of influence in the business arena.

To achieve this requires more than business acumen. It requires spiritual revelation. It requires the same kind of understanding that Jesus had. It requires a special kind of insight—one that Jesus clearly exhibited when He prayed all night and then chose His disciples. This is the protocol of the spiritual realm. This kind of praying provides access to the wisdom of God. It allows us to receive strategies from God that are unprecedented. It allows us to benefit from the wisdom of God.

Selflessness

I have also counseled with many couples in times of crisis in marriage. From this I have discovered that for most who end up in divorce what had been lacking was an apostolic culture of selflessness. Of course there are those also who started marriage on a wrong foundation with tragic consequences later, but for the bulk of those who should know better, the challenge was a lack of understanding of selflessness as a virtue. In reality, this virtue comes with long hours of sustained prayer. When this happens, our flesh is subdued, our spirits are stronger and more willing and flexible to do what is right for the success of the marriage.

Too often we choose business partners, make decisions about marriage, employ people, start enterprises, and make other big decisions just because we feel right about it at the time. We don't take time to pray, not to talk of spending an extended period of time praying before making the decision. If Jesus spent all night praying, we have no business making important decisions doing anything less than He did. We must bring a commensurate sense of importance and dependence on God into major decisions that we make.

If you are embarking on anything of significant magnitude, you need to pray it through even if it means spending all night praying. The apostles Jesus appointed went on to be the vanguard of the church. They laid the foundation of what became the church. Paul would later articulate the role of the apostolic office by saying we are built upon the foundations of the apostles and prophets, Jesus Christ being the Chief Cornerstone (see Eph. 2:20). Therefore, those who would lay the foundation of Jesus' church had to be chosen following the assuring pathway of prayer. No less a pathway could be chosen for a task of such enormity. This is the way Jesus chose to appoint His leaders. Not only did they go on to build the foundations of the church, they communicated the lifestyle and doctrine for the early disciples to follow. Jesus placed a high premium on spending long hours in the presence of God.

ANOTHER REALM OF GRACE

The challenge we face is how to occupy our time if we are going to be spending extended periods in prayer. Some people divide the night into segments of intercession, personal prayer, thanksgiving and praise unto God, worship, an exhortation, and then possibly more prayer. Others spend the time ministering to the needs of the people in intercession and deliverance. However, these examples focus on corporate prayer. It is a different ball game when we are praying for extended periods of time alone, which is what Jesus did. To pray for the length of time Jesus prayed, we have to discover the realm of grace that Jesus depended on.

There are some things this kind of praying is not. It is not perfunctory, indeed it cannot be perfunctory. It is unlikely it involves working through a list of points to pray over. To pray all night like Jesus did requires an intimate partnership with the Holy Spirit. Only the Holy Spirit can energize, direct, inform, and anoint anyone to pray the way Jesus did. It would require utilizing the gifts the Holy Spirit has given, especially the gift of speaking in other tongues.

Paul told the Corinthian church that he thanked God that he spoke in tongues more than they did. He did something strange, he boasted about how long he could pray (see 1 Cor. 14:18). To say he spoke in tongues more than they did, Paul was stressing the fact that there is much to be said for speaking for extended periods of time. To embark on "project praying" therefore, we must become comfortable with speaking in tongues for long periods of time. Nevertheless, praying all night can be wearisome, but I believe it's better to be weary on an assured path. It will no doubt take its toll, but when we remember it's just for a night or few nights, we can persevere.

I remember years ago in 1996 we had just started a new church in London. Our passion was for this church to become a multicultural church impacting every stratum in the city. We were also in the middle of organizing activities to reach different segments of the society. One particular plan was to organize lunchtime meetings in the banking and legal center of London. Our lunchtime meetings soon attracted bankers and lawyers. Some drew closer and became part of everything else we were doing.

However, the secret behind our successful lunchtime meetings was the many occasions when we spent all night praying. Our praying led to an English lady joining one of our evening meetings at the church. She was bowled over by the passion and the evidence of different gifts of the Holy Spirit in operation. As she fellowshipped with us, she wanted us to reach her colleagues in the banking and legal sectors in London so they could become part of what she had come to know—and so the lunchtime fellowship was born. This lunchtime fellowship led to a wonderful time of building a cross-cultural fellowship in the heart of the city. We needed to pray like Jesus for a certain kind of result to follow. At the time there was no fellowship that I can recall in the heart of the city with the kind of cross-cultural mix of people that joined us.

The year before, a team of leaders from my local church went off to Denmark to start a church. In this case, things were a little different. A Danish man in our local church in Nigeria wanted help to take the message of Christ to his family and friends in Denmark. When they arrived in Denmark, they stayed in a hotel for days praying night and day. About a week later, they organized a dinner in honor of our Danish friend. This simple dinner event gave birth to a multicultural church. Most of those in attendance that evening would form the nucleus of the church that was established in Denmark, which I would later oversee. These are ample testimonies to the power of sustained prayer.

In London and Copenhagen, we recognized that for us to break through the cultural barrier as non-Europeans, we needed the power and wisdom of God that came through a sustained long-haul prayer effort. We needed the power of God to break through every kind of barrier that the enemy erects in the name of culture, race, or class, and we needed the wisdom of God to utilize the right strategies that would present the compelling message of Jesus Christ. This prayer strategy has never failed.

There are certain dimensions of Kingdom expression that require us to hunker down and maintain a sustained prayer effort over a period of time. Any individual or church desiring to change existing cultural patterns or superimpose the Kingdom of God on existing structures must approach the task at hand with a commensurate measure of sustained praying.

Cultures, traditions, mindsets, and paradigms are deep-seated positions that can stand in the way of advancing God's Kingdom in our lives and communities. Constructing the new Kingdom culture requires the ushering of a dimension of God's grace that not only changes the hearts of men and women but also propels them to confront their settled cultures and traditions.

Denmark, for instance, is a country with a long Christian history. Martin Luther's reforms were so successful that the predominant denomination is the Lutheran church. So here we were as Nigerians with a very recent Christian history but going forth as missionaries to reevangelize the Danes. This was previously unheard of! Without a doubt we needed to overcome major cultural and racial barriers. Since Jesus went about establishing a new culture of the Kingdom, we are in like fashion expected by God to establish a new culture of the Kingdom of God.

At the heart of this kind of praying is the power to cause a migration or transition in the lives of people such that they live above earthbound traditions. When Jesus chose 12 men out of the disciples who followed Him, it was important to Jesus, I believe, to select men who would lay the groundwork for a global move of God. He couldn't afford to select men who would truncate, or worse still, abort the move of God that was intended to spread throughout the earth. After His resurrection, Jesus reminded the disciples of their worldwide cross-cultural assignment starting from Jerusalem unto Judea, Samaria, and unto the ends of the earth. Left alone, some of the disciples would never have ventured out of Jerusalem.

A few years ago I visited the God Embassy Church in Ukraine led by Pastor Sunday Adelaja. This church is probably the most successful example of a cross-cultural church. Pastor Sunday Adelaja is Nigerian and the church is over 90 percent Ukrainian. We found that they are very committed to long prayer initiatives—every week they have a prayer vigil. Clearly this kind of commitment has born fruit in a very unique way.

My focus on cross-cultural churches may give the impression that this is the only thing we learn from Jesus' commitment to prayer. That's not my intention; if anything, my intention is to give an example of something considered insurmountable, which was overcome through the power of prayer. The inspiration for us is that just as Jesus rising from a prayer vigil chose those who would run with the baton after Him, we also must deal with the most important issues rising up from long hours of sustained prayer.

I cannot overstate the fact that too often we have approached challenges, assignments, tasks, ministries, or the impact of our ministry in our communities, and dare I say nations, without paying the appropriate price in prayer. This is the single, best example Jesus sets for us—that nothing of significance is achieved except when there is the requisite passion and commitment to pray.

CHAPTER **8**

Extending Our Spheres of Influence

Ask of Me, and I will give You the nations for Your inheritance and the ends of the earth for Your possession (Psalm 2:8).

The Lord said to my Lord, "Sit at My right hand, till I make Your enemies Your footstool." The Lord shall send the rod of Your strength out of Zion. Rule in the midst of Your enemies (Psalm 110:1-2).

Psalm 2:8 (above) is awe inspiring in breadth and scope. It refers prophetically to Jesus' triumph and reign on the throne of David. It refers to the awesome majesty and power of God who, by decree and executive fiat, bestows ownership, dominion, and authority over the nations of the earth upon His son. This Psalm has added prophetic potency for the sons of God. We recognize that the rights and privileges of the firstborn son have also been granted to us who are joint heirs with Jesus.

In fact, the entirety of Psalm 2 presents a basis for the sons of God to have dominion on earth and to enthrone the unyielding supremacy of God's sovereignty over demonic hosts and powers. So this Psalm addresses every believer. It is not meant for some with a special relationship with God. There are many who believe that the only time prayer is focused on kingship and dominion is when the "prayer warriors" are praying. However, this is the minimum requirement for us. As the offspring of God, the earth is our inheritance.

God loves the nations of the earth and their diverse cultures. This is why Paul, writing to the Romans, said, "Through Him we have received grace and apostleship for obedience to the faith among all nations..." (Rom. 1:5). Jesus commissions us to go into all the earth and make disciples of all nations for His name.

Paul in Athens describing God to the people of Athens said:

> He has made from one blood every nation of men to dwell on all the face of the earth, and has determined their preappointed times and the boundaries of their dwellings (Acts 17:26).

All these Scriptures underline the importance of nations to God. In another place, the psalmist declares:

> The heaven, even the heavens, are the Lord's; but the earth,
> He has given to the children of men (Psalm 115:16).

Not only does God love the nations, He has entrusted the earth to us! Therefore the real measure of God's manifest sovereignty over the earth is expressed to the degree that we have measurable discernible influence in our homes, communities, cities, and ultimately our nations. It is vital that we recognize our critical roles on the earth as they concern God's purpose.

EXTENDING HIS KINGDOM

From a spiritual perspective, territory is not only geographic it can also represent sectors of human interaction politically, economically, and socially. Therefore I could seek to take territory in a sector of the economy because I want to run a business that would represent the values of the

Kingdom of God in the marketplace. Or I may decide that I want to impact children with the values of the Kingdom of God and consequently seek to take territory in the education sector.

To be effective in extending the frontiers of His Kingdom into any of these territories, I need to first be effective in the place of prayer. I need to go to God with my requests because He says "Ask of Me"! (See John 16:24; Mark 11:24.) Our posture when asking is prayerful. We are deliberate with our words because He desires that we ask. So we ask because the full measure of our asking is the nations and the ends of the earth. It is a blank cheque from God. Therefore with our hearts filled with faith, we ask.

This fact may seem somewhat remote from the daily realities of life, but nevertheless it is true. And so to the person who chooses prayerfully to discover its awesome power, your life will never be the same.

For instance, in the past three years we have been involved in an intensive effort of extending the frontiers of God's Kingdom into some of the worst slum dwellings in Lagos. As mentioned previously, this has involved going into areas with some of the worst criminals in Lagos. We knew we could not just go in and expect to bring change if we hadn't first gained spiritual ascendancy and supremacy. We had to first bind the strongman and then we could plunder his goods.

Many of these neighborhoods are very scary because violence could erupt at a moment's notice and we didn't go in armed or with police. I remember one occasion when I led a team into a slum dwelling in Ijora. Anything could have happened to us! For a start, the pimps didn't like our presence—we were bad for business. But our decrees had gone ahead of us and we had superimposed God's Kingdom upon the area. Our words and our posture in prayer was that of kings decreeing the rule of God's Kingdom in all the places we entered. This position had a very clear, visible impact wherever we went. Drug dealers, pimps, owners of brothels, and leaders of street gangs responded to us as deliverers who brought hope and change. It was amazing!

Clearly the reason for our success was tied to the fact that in extending the frontier of God's Kingdom we were actively dethroning principalities and powers exercising influence and control over the areas we entered. Our influence has grown to the point where the police have on occasion invited us to help them. This is the amazing power of prayer focused on extending the frontiers of God's rulership.

When we pray to God with these words, our prayers and even our body language take on an authoritative mien. Our words carry the weight of God's desire and expectation. In other words our words carry gravitas. Mundane concerns of life, as important as they are, cannot distract us. We recognize the high call of God that energizes our hearts such that these words are not just words of prayer any more but divine decrees. We are responding to God in a manner in which He desires. We are actually bringing words to Him that He expressly requests from us. Angelic assistance is summoned in this kind of prayer because we are enforcing a return to ancient landmarks over God's earth and the nations whose boundaries He has established.

TERRITORIAL PRAYERS

When we pray in this manner our focus is territorial. As believers we must recognize that every sphere of human endeavor has demonic hosts assigned to control it and use it as a platform for wickedness and pervasion. So don't be fooled by the prevalence of different types of evil in our cities! Each time I travel, I am reminded that demonic hosts of hell want a city that is veering toward anarchy, while we are fighting to enthrone God's Kingdom. I have observed that different cities have different spiritual atmospheres. Some cities are on the verge of disorder. Others may seem very orderly but lack warmth and friendliness. Others promote lewdness and sensuality. Therefore, prayer is a God-given tool for displacing demonic hosts that define each territory.

Every believer must recognize, as Paul said in Ephesians 6:12, "that we wrestle not against flesh and blood but against *principalities, powers, rulers of darkness* and *spiritual wickedness* in heavenly places." Each of these four categorizations of demonic hosts underscores a contention over who would rule. *Principalities* reflect control over a geographically defined area; *powers* connote authority and the ability to subjugate; *rulers of darkness* connote a certain ranking of authority assigned to propagate principles of satan; and, *spiritual wickedness* refers to false religions that influence and lead people astray under the cloak of spirituality. From the words of Paul we recognize that our wrestling first is not against human beings.

Second, we recognize that our wrestling is actually against the elite rulership cadre of the kingdom of darkness. Third, we recognize that this wrestling is not optional. Taking territory is at the heart of the Kingdom agenda which is dominion! Every believer is expected to have a sphere of influence. This requirement is tied to God's original plan for humankind in Genesis. In addition, our status after redemption is as kings and priests. No king has real authority without a domain or area over which he exercises rulership.

Today we have much territory to retake. On every front much territory awaits in education, media, entertainment, politics, government, and business. One key territory to reclaim is what I call the cultural mandate. This spans such critical areas as entertainment, music, art, and media. These areas are critical because they are key influencers of societal behavior, ethics, ambitions, and icons.

The heroes of our faith and their historical context present us with a rich heritage for communicating the right cultural values. But nobody ventures out to take this kind of territory without first taking the territory in the spiritual realm. It is first in the spiritual realm that the battle is won.

Every believer must exercise this power to extend the frontiers of God's Kingdom. When Paul arrived in Ephesus, he met 12 disciples. Thereafter for two years he trained them at a place called the school of Tyranus. After this period of training, Paul and these disciples spread the gospel of Jesus Christ to all of Asia. This was the result of what Paul and 12 disciples committed themselves to do. Their impact was so pervasive that it affected the economy and the worship of the local goddess, Diana. Miracles and healings abounded. Those who had practiced magic brought their books to be burnt. Such was the scale of their impact that it caused great alarm in the city of Ephesus! At one point, the followers of Diana went on the counter offensive. For two hours they cried out with one voice saying, "Great is Diana of the Ephesians!"

Sustained prayer was the key to the success Paul and the disciples experienced in Ephesus. This is why, when Paul wrote to the believers at Ephesus, he exhorted them to pray always with all prayer and supplication in the Spirit, being watchful in the business of prayer. This exhortation was the result of his experience at Ephesus.

The Kingdom of God advances as we pray. My heartfelt passionate desire is that as you read this book you will be filled with revelation of God's desire for you to take much territory. Not only that, but you will embark on this prayer adventure using the matchless power of prayer to rise on eagle's wings and blossom as a child of destiny.

RISING ABOVE MEDIOCRITY

And the Lord spoke to Moses, saying, "Send men to spy out the land of Canaan, which I am giving to the children of Israel; from each tribe of their fathers you shall send a man, every one a leader among them (Numbers 13:1-2).

When the children of Israel were on the threshold of the Promised Land, God instructed them to send spies ahead to survey the land and bring back a report. Moses requested that they bring back a report on the nature of the land; its inhabitants, whether they were tall or short; its geography; and, fruitfulness. The spies who were sent to survey the land were the elite of the children of Israel. They were specially chosen from the ranks of the leadership of each of the tribes of Israel. Each one was notable for qualities of leadership.

When they returned from spying the land over a 40-day period, of the 12 spies, ten were of the opinion that the land of promise could not really be the land of promise. The reasons offered: although the land truly "flowed with milk and honey," they said the people were strong, the cities fortified, the land devours its inhabitants, and they felt as small if they were grasshoppers compared to the giants who lived there (see Num. 13:33). The perspective of the ten spies was if it was truly the land of promise, then the people in the land should be weak and not strong, the cities should be exposed and not be fortified. This perspective dealt a death blow to their ability to prepare for and receive what God had ordained for them. They forgot the parting injunction of Moses to "Be of good courage" (Num. 13:20).

Can you imagine the tragedy of leadership that is not visionary? This was the crowning glory of the journey of these leaders through the wilderness. Rather than being strengthened by their wilderness experience, they rather developed a stunted, mediocre approach to the defining moments of their lives when the time to take the Promised Land presented itself.

On the other hand, two spies—Joshua and Caleb—had a different perspective. They quieted the voices of doubt and unbelief and proclaimed, "Let us go up at once and take possession, for we are well able to overcome it" (Num. 13:30). Yet the ten spies said, "We are not able to go up against the people, for they are stronger than we" (Num. 13:31). Perhaps because they were more in number, their unbelief tipped the balance and the entire congregation of Israel wept and bemoaned their lot in the wilderness.

Yet Joshua and Caleb would not give up. They tore their clothes and once more tried to rouse the people in faith saying, "The land we passed through to spy out is an exceedingly good land. If the Lord delights in us, then He will bring us into this land and give it to us" (Num. 14:7-8). They warned the people that their unbelief was tantamount to rebelling against God, pointing out the people were bread for the taking since their protection had departed from them. What was their reward for this great exhortation? The threat of being stoned to death!

Prophetic Perspective

The tragic consequence of this tumultuous sequence of events was that every adult who embarked upon the journey from Egypt to the Promised Land died in the wilderness—except Caleb and Joshua, the two spies who gave a positive report. The questions that agitate my mind: Why would ten leaders have such a wrong perspective of the promises of God? Why did they think because the people in the land were strong and the cities fortified that it would be impossible for them to dispossess the inhabitants? Why was their mentality unable to grasp the fact God was the possessor of the heavens and the earth and that whatever He promised He could give?

One major challenge confronting the ten spies was the fact that they had a *wrong prophetic perspective*. They could not see what God was seeing or they could not feel the heartbeat of God on the matter. To be prophetic is to feel the pulse of God. To be prophetic is to discern the will of God in a matter. To be prophetic is to sense the direction of God. Tragically they were ruled by their senses. When they saw the giants and the fortified cities, fear gripped their hearts and they spread this same fear to an entire nation.

To see as God sees is to seek God in the place of prayer. The man or woman who stays consistently in the presence of God begins to have clarity of sight and vision. An accurate perspective becomes the natural consequence of being totally God-centered. When Habakkuk received the burden of the Lord and ministered to the nation of Judah in a time of great calamity and in the midst of Habakkuk's burden and God's response, Habakkuk declares, "I will stand my watch and set myself on the rampart, and watch to see what He will say to me" (Hab. 2:1). Habakkuk's posture was one of prayer. To *watch* is to seek God prayerfully. Habakkuk was assured that so long as he stood his watch, God would speak.

And the joy of all those who stand their watch is to hear God speak. For when God speaks, His word comes forth as a light that shines in a dark place. His word pierces through the darkness of fear, doubt, and insecurities bringing comfort, assurance, and direction. This is why Joshua and Caleb said, "if the Lord delights in us." They understood the big issue was God's delight that they possess the land of Canaan. It was God who requested that they send spies to the land to bring back a good report, which was meant to bolster the nation in readiness for what was waiting for them.

When Jehoshaphat was faced with the armies of Ammon, Moab, and Mount Seir massing against Judah, fear tore through his spirit. He was king of Judah and Benjamin, two out of the twelve tribes of Israel. He was ruler over a small nation. But Jehoshaphat did the wisest thing in the circumstances. He sought God with prayer and fasting and gathered the entire nation to do the same. Jehoshaphat could have buckled under with fear, but he chose to seek God. What a wise decision he made in the circumstances! This decision made all the difference. As he sought God, a word came through Jahaziel one of the Levites (see 2 Chron. 20:14-15). Oh what a joy when we hear from God in the midst of adversity! It makes all the difference. In Jehoshaphat's case, the entire nation was of one accord in prayer, fasting, and most importantly in its united stand of faith. The nation took to heart the word of God and saw the deliverance of God.

Caleb and Joshua knew that the protection of the Canaanites had departed from them. They had spiritual insight which made them understand this fact. This insight could only have come from intimacy with God.

Seek God's Agenda

This story of the spies presents a timeless example of the challenges we face every day on every front. Do we succumb to doubt and unbelief? Are we full of low self-esteem in the face of the odds we grapple with every day? I recall years ago arriving in Denmark as a missionary. I felt so inadequate, wondering what message I had for the people. They all seemed so self-sufficient while I was in my own eyes an economically disadvantaged Nigerian sent to preach to a small, wealthy nation. Fortunately my sense of inadequacy drove me into the presence of God. The more I prayed, the more God spoke to me affirming me as His voice in the land of Denmark to dethrone principalities and powers.

Prayerfully seeking God's agenda is the key to assuring our future! Our future is in the hands of God, but can He trust our perspective well enough to invite us to survey what He has in store for us? God desires us to be prophetic in order that we spy the future accurately and prepare for it. The risk is we can destroy our future and the future of those who follow us if our perspective is wrong! Our focus in prayer is of vital importance. This is a challenge for most believers because our prayer is focused most times on what we perceive as our need or the problems or challenges we need to overcome. It is as though we cannot trust God sufficiently to say that our primary focus is God's agenda. However, it is this reengineering of our prayer focus that opens up another dimension of God's grace allowing us to spy what is ahead and respond appropriately.

My prayer is that like Jesus you will say, "My food is to do the will of Him who sent me, and to finish His work" (John 4:34).

Recently some of us have been praying concerning Nigeria's political and economic well-being. As we have prayed, we have sensed God ask, "Who will go for Me? Whom shall I send?" It is easy for us to stay in our comfort zone and continue praying endlessly. But our praying must lead us to the point where our response is, "Here I am Lord, send me!"

When we hear God asking, "Whom shall I send?" What will our response be? Will it be that the giants of politics and corruption are too big for us to handle? The political landscape in Nigeria, as I believe in much of the world, is certainly complex and can be treacherous and unpredictable. For instance in Nigeria, many politicians seeking office know they will have to contend with rigging, violence, and intimidation. This can scare away many well-meaning believers with a desire for advancing the Kingdom of God from venturing into politics. However, in the timetable of God, this is the season to enter this arena and reconcile it to God. I hear the trumpet blasts calling the army of God to the battle lines in this critical area.

CHAPTER 9

Give God No Rest

*For Zion's sake I will not hold my peace, and for Jerusalem's sake **I will not rest**, until her righteousness goes forth as brightness, and her salvation as a lamp that burns* (Isaiah 62:1).

*I have set watchmen upon your walls, O Jerusalem; they shall never hold their peace day or night. You who make mention of the Lord, do not keep silent, and **give Him no rest** till He establishes and till He makes Jerusalem a praise in the earth* (Isaiah 62:6-7).

In December 1994 we had just entered a season of intense prayer and accelerated missionary activity. Unbelievably within a year, we had planted churches in Britain, Germany, Jamaica, and another was planned for Washington, DC. In our local assembly in Lagos we had just concluded a prayer workshop with the theme "Give Him No Rest." Most of us had been praying more than ever! We were getting accustomed to spending hours praying with passion. The words "pray without ceasing" were becoming a way of life. Moreover as we prayed, it was as though we were infusing life into a flowering plant. In every direction we could see much fruit. New churches were also being planted in Nigeria, too.

Most of us involved in all this activity had only really begun our work with the Lord two or three years prior. The size of our congregation was growing and we soon had multiple services with attendance near 7,000 adults. The community of praying men and women surged to over 300. It was truly a time of blessed growth and diversity. Our spiritual antennae were heightened. There was a sense of urgency that accompanied everything we were doing. We wanted to go to the ends of the earth. Our passion was driven by the words "give Him no rest." It was mind-blowing to think that God asks us to trouble Him ceaselessly. What a command! What a discovery! This revelation was so different from our traditional view of God. We discovered that as much as we were to revere God, we were also to trouble Him ceaselessly. Remember, God can never be wearied. As the prophet Isaiah declared:

> *Have you not known? Have you not heard? The everlasting God, the Lord, the Creator of the ends of the earth, neither faints nor is weary. His understanding is unsearchable* (Isaiah 40:28).

God is limitless in strength and power. This is why we are exhorted to give Him no rest.

I remember as a child I wearied my parents on many occasions with my many requests. I recall one instance when I was 14 years old and we were on vacation in Holland. I wanted to buy something in every shop we entered. When I didn't get my way, I sulked. But I wearied them so often that many times they just got me what I wanted in order to stop my whining.

However with God, we are confident to give Him no rest because He says, "I will not rest." What is impossible for men is possible with God (see Matt. 19:26). While it may be considered rude and even wicked not to give our colleagues any rest, it is a completely different case when it comes to God. I wonder how many times we have given up in the place of prayer when as far as God is concerned we must take on the attitude of ensuring He has no rest. I see in my mind's eye an image of God in a vexed and restless state determined to see the church shine brightly in righteousness. This picture shows God displaying a high degree of personal commitment to see His desire come to pass on earth. Whenever God commits to a matter, we are assured of full and complete victory.

In Isaiah 62:6-7, the prophet Isaiah declares:

> *I have set watchmen on your walls, O Jerusalem; they shall never hold their peace day or night. You who make mention of the Lord, do not keep silent, and **give Him no rest** till He establishes and till He makes Jerusalem a praise in the earth.*

These two verses are loaded with prophetic symbols. The *watchmen* are those who want to watch in the place of prayer for Jerusalem. *Jerusalem* here symbolically represents the universal Church that must become *"a praise in the earth,"* the attractive centerpiece of God. So when God says He has "set watchmen" on the walls of Jerusalem who will not hold their peace day or night, we see that God has established a partnership with the watchmen. What an amazing partnership!

A Partnership

The first point we must understand is that watchmen were not a special breed of people. The only qualification for being a watchman was and still remains a willingness to share the same passion and desires of God. Everywhere the eyes of the Lord are going to and fro over the face of the earth looking for those who share His passion. When He finds them, He commissions them into a ministry of ceaseless, unyielding prayer.

These Scriptures reveal the unshakeable power of divine partnership—a partnership to establish a permanent gateway between Heaven and earth. The unmistakable result of this partnership has been defined— the Church becoming praise in the earth. When the Church is praise in the earth, what are the signs that define it as such? These are righteousness, integrity, compassion, influence, truth, power, healing, and peace.

Until this happens, wherever the name of Jesus is exalted, we fall short of God's expectation.

God is restoring revelation of the apostolic foundations upon which His Church is to be built. Without these foundations, the Church will be weak and anemic. But when the Church is built upon the right foundation of revelation, it becomes the house on the rock that stands against every onslaught of the enemy and it makes its advance forcefully.

I pray that all around the world this understanding will act as a clarion waking up many to accept the challenge to stay upon the walls of the places of influence they ought to conquer in divine partnership with God.

THE POWER OF OUR WORDS

By faith we understand that the worlds were framed by the word of God, so that the things which are seen were not made of the things which are visible (Hebrews 11:3).

Everything God created came about through the spoken word. The account of creation in Genesis chapter 1 reveals the power of God through the spoken word over a six-day period. In Genesis 1:3 we read, "Then God said 'let there be light'; and there was light." In verse 6 God again said, "Let there be a firmament in the midst of the waters, and let it divide the waters from the waters." This process continued for five days until all of the physical representations of the earth had been created.

This is why the writer of the Book of Hebrews describing faith said in chapter 11:3:

By faith we understand that the worlds were framed by the word of God, so that the things which are seen were not made of the things which are visible.

In other words, the power of God's word called forth the earth from the invisible realm of the Spirit. Asaph the psalmist in Psalm 50:1 describes the power of God's speech with these words, "The Mighty One, God the Lord, has spoken and called the earth from the rising of the sun to its going down." Even creation has a voice as another psalmist David in Psalm 19:1-4 says:

> *The heavens declare the glory of God; and the firmament shows His handiwork. Day unto day utters speech, and night unto night reveals knowledge. There is no speech nor language where their voice is not heard. Their line has gone out through all the earth and their words to the end of the world.*

These Scriptures reveal the power of speech in bringing into being that which had not been. When Jesus rode triumphantly into Jerusalem, there were many crying out in praise and worship saying, "Blessed is the King who comes in the name of the Lord! Peace in heaven and glory in the highest!" (Luke 19:38). When the Pharisees asked Jesus to rebuke the disciples for praising Him, Jesus answered, if the disciples kept quiet, the stones would be compelled to cry out in praise unto God (see Luke 19:40).

The Lord said to Jeremiah:

> *…Behold I have put my words in your mouth. See, I have this day set you over the nations and over the kingdoms, to root out and to pull down, to destroy and to throw down, to build and to plant* (Jeremiah 1:9-10).

We see from these various Scriptures that everything God created He gave a voice. But every child of God has been given not just a voice to declare the majesty and glory of God, but a voice that has the power to positively change things on earth. We can root out, pull down, and destroy evil, and we can build or plant godly values, godly families, godly businesses, godly communities, etc. We are unique in the midst of all that God has done. Just as whatever God wanted to see, He created by speaking, so also we have the power to change circumstances by what we speak.

TWO CENTERS OF DOMINION

There are two centers of dominion established by God. First are the heavens and then the earth. This is why Psalm 115:16 declares, "The heaven, even the heavens, are the Lord's; but the earth He has given to the children of men." So God spoke all of creation into existence. As He spoke, the power of His words were translated to something visible representing what was on His mind. We see a link between the words of God and tangible reality.

The words of God carried something invisible that could nevertheless translate to something visible. It is this power of God through the spoken word that we see translated to awesome events like the creation of the heavens and the earth. The same power is available to us on earth. Our speech can make manifest awe-inspiring events through the power of what we say. Prayer, therefore, becomes a licensed authority from God to create circumstances on earth that advance His Kingdom. This is because we are the offspring of God. We are one with God. On earth we are His agents for establishing His thoughts, His desires, and His vision. In these circumstances, our words become potent!

Prayer becomes a powerful tool enabling us to come to God with words. These words fill up the atmosphere with the purpose of God. With this revelation, we begin the process of configuration over our spheres of influence. We become spiritual architects designing and configuring the earth to agree with the design and template of our Father, confident that our words carry weight and glory in the spiritual realm. From this perspective, we embark on the sacred assignment of dominion.

The earth is our sphere of influence. Remember, dominion is our goal. This revelation of prayer excites me to no end. It shows me the limitless power I have with God. It reminds me that I am an extension of God on the earth. Practically speaking I can shape the destiny of my family based on this revelation. My words have power in the spiritual realm. I can change the destiny of children who have strayed into a wayward life by the power of what I speak. I can determine my future in marriage by what I speak. I can shape the course of my ministry by the power of my words in the place of prayer.

What is more, the Bible is a rich resource for words that convey the power of the spiritual realm. It provides me the keys to shaping everything according to the Word of God. There is no context in which the power of what I speak in prayer would not bring change. This is why Jesus said the words that I speak are Spirit and Life. This is one revelation the enemy cannot overcome. What an awesome privilege. Prayer therefore goes beyond what I feel I need or seeking God for a breakthrough in a certain area of my life. As valid as these kinds of prayer are, nevertheless we discover a more powerful role of prayer in our lives. I therefore take time to read, assimilate, and even memorize Scripture so that my words are lethal—not just in repeating Scripture but in shaping my environment to reflect the Kingdom of God.

Speaking Silences the Enemy

Our speaking also silences the enemy. It puts a stop to the accusing words of the enemy. The psalmist declares in Psalm 8:2:

> *Out of the mouth of babes and nursing infants You have ordained strength, because of Your enemies, that You may silence the enemy and the avenger.*

When we speak, the enemy loses his voice. Too often we are distracted by all the noise and activity in the world that makes it look as though we are in a losing battle. But this is because we are not busy silencing the enemy with our words. We can put a stop to the voice of the enemy. In too many homes, the enemy's voice is very strong, leading marriages astray. If only husbands and wives would start speaking, because God says *out of the mouth of babes and nursing infants He has ordained strength.*

Too often we forget this fact. It amazes me the investment we make in leisure activity but when the chips are down, we behave like ordinary men and women. Many homes have the latest gadgets for relaxation and leisure but have no idea how the spiritual realm functions. When trouble comes, they try every kind of analysis without recognizing the fact that we are in a war over who will have dominion.

Jesus has conquered the enemy. The enemy knows this. The angels know this. All of creation knows this, but it is up to the sons and daughters of God to enforce this dominion. When we try to deal with problems through strife and arguments, we show that we are ignorant of how things work in the spiritual realm. It is not strife and arguments He has ordained. If only we would remember this fact. I counsel with many couples having marital problems who are oblivious to the reality of the spiritual realm. They attempt to overwhelm each other with arguments. If only they would seek to overwhelm the enemy instead. This applies to every area of life. The strength of our words is meant to overwhelm the enemy and not to overwhelm each other.

To our spouses and brothers and sisters in Christ our words must be salted with grace and love. We choose our words wisely. We uphold each other with our words. We encourage each other with our words. We celebrate each other with our words. When we face the enemy, we know our words carry strength. This strength mutes the enemy. Sometimes all we have to do is enter our closet and pray in tongues for an hour. When you do so, you discover that at the least you are attempting to do the right thing. You may not have the strength at that point to resolve the issues, but you will have the strength to restrain yourself from doing the wrong thing. This is how we silence the enemy.

Bold as Lions

You may feel the enemy goading you to say something nasty; but as you pray, you are silencing the enemy's voice. When we have this revelation, we stop complaining about circumstances as though we are victims. We are not victims of circumstance but sons and daughters of the Most High God. This fact changes the equation.

Most of the problems people face is because they haven't learned to silence the enemy. When problems come, we look in the wrong place for solutions. I know many couples who look to their parents or their friends for help. This is not bad in itself, but it displays a lack of spiritual understanding. I meet many believers who are spiritually weak and anemic because they don't speak.

Finally, the consequence of not speaking is to become ineffective through our silence. So rather than impose silence on the enemy, the enemy imposes silence on us. This is the tragedy many of us face—silence in our homes and silence in our communities. A Christianity that lacks power is an impotent Christianity. This is not what God ordained for us. Unfortunately, too many people have become accustomed to the wrong view of prayer that is focused on coming to God with a begging bowl rather than silencing the voice of the enemy. It is time to embrace our future with assertiveness and boldness that is our heritage. Prayer is the activity of the bold for "the righteous are bold as a lion" (Prov. 28:1).

When we pray in tongues, we also come with words unto God, but this time we come with words that in the realm of the Spirit are a mystery. God has given us a language that is a mystery. Only God understands this language and of course anyone to whom the Holy Spirit has granted the gift of interpretation of tongues. Now when I speak in a language that is known to men, the language has all the features that are common to languages such as punctuation, sentences, etc.

In the same way, when we speak in unknown tongues, we speak words that also have all the features of a language. When we speak in tongues, we have the vast resource of a language given to us by the Holy Spirit. One of the reasons the Holy Spirit gives us this language is because of our limited vocabulary in the languages we have learned to express the creative power of God within us. When you hear someone proficient in more than one language, sometimes they struggle to express themselves and switch to a language they are more comfortable with.

For instance, in Nigeria, the average person speaks English as a second language. Though they maybe proficient in English, they may find that sometimes when expressing themselves in prayer they revert to the language they first learned to speak. Even at that, no matter how eloquent we may be, we are still limited in expressing as fully as we should what

God seeks to achieve on earth. This is when the language of the Holy Spirit comes and fills our mouths with words that are expressions of the creative power of God resident in us. As I speak in tongues, my words are pregnant with the power to configure things, to change the atmosphere, and to still the mouth of the enemy.

A Deeper Dimension

When I add to my speaking sensitivity to the Holy Spirit, it opens up a deeper dimension of the power of the words I speak. Sometimes I may start praying in tongues and my language initially is very repetitive. This may go on for 15 to 30 minutes. Also when I pray in tongues my mind maybe wandering all over the place thinking about any and everything. Other times I may start and find that from the moment I open my mouth to pray, there is a gushing forth of tongues expressed with vigor, vitality, and power—and this could go on for an hour more sometimes reaching a thundering crescendo especially when praying with others.

In the first example, that type of repetitive praying is usually the process of edification because for all sorts of reasons when we come before the Lord to pray, we need to be edified. We need the spiritual building process that strengthens and invigorates our inner spirit. In such a context, as we continue to pray, our inner self is edified and our sensitivity to the Holy Spirit should increase as well. This increased sensitivity is also expressed in a widening and deepening of our vocabulary. When we pray like this, we are subject to the stirring of the Holy Spirit. The tongues we speak as we pray are a direct product of what the Holy Spirit seeks to do. Sometimes our speaking may address a knotty issue that needs to be resolved in a home. At other times it might be the need to displace principalities and powers that are entrenched in a community, city, or region.

This introduces a dimension of the limitless power of God through prayer. So, for instance, if you find it difficult to memorize Scripture or you feel you are not very eloquent in a learned language, then switch to the unknown tongues or language given by the Holy Spirit. This is why Paul said to the Corinthian Christians that, "I thank my God I speak in tongues more than you all" (see 1 Cor. 14:18).

AVAILED VESSELS

The more we speak in tongues, the greater we avail the Holy Spirit of ourselves as vessels through whom He can release the hidden treasures of God spoken in a mystery. This has a double impact on the devil. Not only does the devil not have the power to resist our words, the import of what we speak is lost on him. So our speaking in tongues becomes like a second oar we have to release the creative power of words on earth.

As a result of this revelation, I can speak in tongues for hours sometimes up to four hours at a time because there is so much I need to focus the creative power of God in redressing. Living in Nigeria I see so much the creative power of God can address. When I think of the fact that in God's eyes the minimum every believer should seek to attain is greatness, I am motivated to pray in this manner, especially when believers sit in churches exercising themselves to no end merely with housekeeping duties masquerading as ministry. I think of the idle capacity wasting away in churches while the society is groaning in pain waiting for the manifestation of the children of God. Thinking about it alone motivates me to pray for hours.

When I think of the awesome role of the Church in every nation to bring transformation and wholesomeness, I can pray in this manner for hours until I see this come to pass. When I think of the ravages of corruption that have laid waste two or three generations of Nigerians, I can pray in this manner for hours. When I think of the decimation of Nigerian youth through poor educational facilities, cultism, and exploitation by the political class, I can pray in this manner for hours. This truly is the awesome privilege of prayer. It is the foundation for every kind of change we desire to see wherever we live.

Dispelling the Darkness

I hear my friends in Europe complain about all sorts of problems, which they describe as being part of the humanist agenda. One example of this agenda many would say is the recognition of homosexual marriages. Added to this is the fact that it is now illegal in some countries to speak against homosexuality. But this is not the main issue because so long as we have the sin nature it will yield fruit in all kinds of ways.

The antidote to the sin nature is godliness. How do we receive all things that pertain to life and godliness? It is through Jesus, but we know the god of this age has blinded the eyes of many not to receive Jesus. How do we dispel the darkness that blinds many? It is only in the place of prayer that this can be done. So rather than fight what I see, I take my focus to the unseen realm of the spirit with the creative power of God to transform and enthrone the godly heritage I desire. This requires discipline and tenacity because we are dealing with uprooting entrenched positions of hegemony occupied by the prince over the power of the air (the devil) and his cohorts.

My prayer is that God would raise men and women with godly passion and zeal who will take this revelation of the transformative power of God to uproot the agenda of principalities and powers in their cities, regions, and nations. This is the power reserved for the sons and daughters of the Most High God. Any philosophy or way of life that is contrary to the Word of God must first be dealt with in the realm of the spirit. What we face is not flesh and blood but principalities, powers, rulers of darkness, and spiritual wickedness in heavenly places.

Prayer alone does not solve problems. What it does is lay God's spiritual foundation for change to come. What it does is displace principalities and powers entrenched over cities and nations so the Kingdom of God may truly advance. Advancing in the natural with activist agendas only ends in strife. In the natural, our disposition is love and compassion. In the natural, our words are salted with grace. In the natural, we are peacemakers.

We are the sons and daughters of God with the high call of God. Anyone in the Kingdom has only one call! It is the high call of God! The high call of God is to master the earth and show proof to principalities and powers that we live and function in the knowledge of the fact that Jesus spoiled principalities and powers making an open show of them. Every believer around the globe whether in the United States, China, Britain, Nigeria, Saudi Arabia, Iran, or wherever else has a distinctive heritage. It doesn't matter whether you are an old or young Christian. All that matters is accepting this privilege with childlike faith.

This is why Christianity is so unique. It is the free gift of God. To as many as believe He gives the right to become children of God. It is God who gives. You may never have prayed in a learned language or in tongues for more than five minutes in your life. But this doesn't stop you from accepting and functioning in the power God has bestowed upon you. All you need to do is embrace this revelation with childlike faith. It is the free gift of God. Therefore:

> *Let the saints be joyful in glory; let them sing aloud on their beds. Let the high praises of God be in their mouth, and a two-edged sword in their hand, to execute vengeance on the nations, and punishment on the peoples; to bind their kings with chains, and their nobles with fetters of iron; to execute on them the written judgment—this honor have all His saints* (Psalm 149:5-9).

This glorious Scripture describing the triumphant posture of the saints of God in executing God's righteous judgment on the nations ends with the words, *"this honor have all His saints."* It is an *honor* God has bestowed on us. Not according to our works but according to His righteousness. The only thing we can bring is faith.

Chapter 10

Leading From the Front

I thank my God I speak with tongues more than you all
(1 Corinthians 14:18).

Paul boasted to the Corinthians that he could speak in tongues more than all of them. What a boast to make! Paul said this to the Corinthians at a time when he was seeking to bring order to their lives. Paul's statement tells us something—leaders lead from the front especially when it comes to prayer. Astonishingly, many pastors find themselves subject to witchcraft because they don't lead from the front in prayer. The quality of leadership in a local assembly is tied to the quality of leadership the pastors first provide in prayer. Leadership in prayer is one assignment that cannot be delegated. Even though the pastor may not lead every prayer meeting, it must be obvious that the pastor leads spiritually—evident in his leadership in the place of prayer.

This is not only true for pastors it is equally true for heads of ministries, business people, teachers, parents, etc. If you are in any leadership role and you are not at the forefront of prayer, you are shortchanging yourself and those you lead. When Paul wrote his dissertation on speaking in tongues, it was a bold statement to proclaim to the Corinthians that he could speak in tongues more than every Corinthian believer. This could be mistaken for arrogance. But Paul wasn't arrogant, he was underscoring the importance of speaking in other tongues even as he was dealing with the pressing problem of a church sorely in need of order.

Whatever you do, it is imperative that you lead from the front in prayer. Husbands especially need to lead from the front in prayer. Many husbands think it is the wife's responsibility to be the watchman of the home. This is wrong. The husband is the head of the home. Therefore, just as Jesus who is the Head of the Church lives forevermore to make intercession for the Church, so also husbands as the head of their homes must lead as advocates leading in intercession for their homes before God.

You may head a ministry in church and believe that it is the job of the prayer department to carry the burdens of your department. This is also wrong. Everyone in a leadership role must lead the prayer effort. I meet heads of ministries who complain to no end about the lack of commitment of the people they lead. Some get bitter and disillusioned. However, I have found from experience that if you carry the burden of your ministry and the people God brings to you in the place of prayer, you will certainly see change.

Some years ago I was appointed the resident pastor of my church. Before this occasion, I had served in many other leadership roles. This was at a time when our local assembly was setting up missions in some of the worst slum dwellings in the city of Lagos, as mentioned previously. Many in leadership went to the field and many others either joined the mission effort or left because the senior pastor was on a missions sabbatical. It was despairing that Sunday services had a despondent air because many felt that with the senior pastor away, the church would not survive. What kept us buoyant in faith and strong in spirit was prayer. I led a team in prayer every Friday night for three months consisting of the prayer community, the worship team, and some other pastors. It inspired many of us because they saw me paying a spiritual price from the front.

When many were tired and wanted to give up, I never gave up. I persevered because I recognized the principle of leading from the front in prayer. A friend of mine who inspires me is a pastor of a church in Newcastle, England. When he started the church, he dedicated 12 hours every Tuesday to pray. He showed by example the quality of his intercession and today they have a thriving multiracial church. Every leader, like Paul, ought to make this boast.

The reason leaders ought to lead in prayer is because they will inspire others to follow and break new ground. Leaders navigate the direction of their people. The strength and quality of a church—organization, business, or home—is determined by the quality of the leadership of the leader in prayer. When you visit some churches you can tell they are nice people. You can tell they love God, but yet you sense something is lacking. Usually in these types of church what is lacking is spiritual clout. They usually lack authority in the spiritual realm. They have no experience of war and taking territory and having influence to bring salvation and discipleship wherever God has placed them.

Now imagine Paul who had earlier made a boast to the Corinthians. When he arrived in Ephesus, Paul took the 12 disciples he found there, and for two and a half years Paul trained them. I believe Paul would have taught them to pray, among other things. When he wrote to them, we see in Ephesians 6:18 Paul's exhortation to pray *"always* with all prayer and supplication in the Spirit, being watchful to this end with all perseverance...."* What a leader Paul was! In that time, all of Asia heard the gospel.

My greatest inspiration to pray came through my pastor. From when I had just given my life to Christ to more recent times, his devotion to prayer has inspired me and also caused me to be an inspiration to others. The greatest calling of leadership is to lead by example. To demonstrate in practical ways what they want others to follow. More than at any other time, this is one aspect of our faith that must be restored to its full glory. What potency we will carry when the church attains this measure of maturity.

Ephesus—A Model Church

Influence and transformation are the keys to reconciling men and cultures to God. The church at Ephesus provides a useful template of how these twin objectives can be achieved by churches worldwide. It is critical to understand that the great commission must involve not just the salvation, discipleship, and commissioning of believers, but of necessity it must include influencing and transforming the institutions of human interaction. As kings and priests of the King of all kings, our role on earth is to seek every opportunity to enthrone the truth and the values of God's Kingdom on every aspect of human society.

The church at Ephesus, therefore, represents possibly the best example of a church seeking to influence and transform all segments of its society in a radical Christ-centered way. It is a model to study because it reveals much about the power of prayer to break down demonic strongholds in a city.

When Paul arrived in Ephesus, he found 12 disciples in the city, and he immediately engaged the disciples with a view to equipping them for service. Paul did not begin to print flyers and run all over the place to bring people to "his church." No, he hunkered down with the 12 disciples. The next thing he did was enquire whether they had received the Holy Spirit baptism. When he found out they had not, Paul prayed for them to receive the Holy Spirit and they did. Thereafter, Paul stayed back with the disciples and trained them over a two and a half year period. Soon it was reported that all of Asia had heard the gospel.

Discipleship

Paul devoted more than two years to these disciples. What an investment. Too many pastors today want to reap where they have not sown. The key to transforming any home, community, environment, workplace, marriage, or city is found in the discipleship of people by the pastors. The pastor's first assignment is to train and not to build structures for increased membership. When people are trained, they will build the structures. God brings all the gifts for building structures as raw material first and then looks to the leaders He puts in place to train those He sends. They in turn build the structures. All of Asia heard after 12 disciples had spent two and a half years with Paul.

Also, there were visible signs of change in the way of thinking as those who had magical books brought them out to be burnt. The commerce of the city was also affected as the worshipers of Diana were turning to Jesus Christ. This had an economic impact as the demand for figurines of the goddess dropped significantly such that blacksmiths in the city were becoming riotous. Things got so heated that at some point when Jason, who was Paul's traveling companion, sought to address the tense crowd, an uproar arose when they discovered he was a Jew, and for the next two hours they chanted, "Great is Diana of the Ephesians" (Acts 19:34).

When Paul at a later stage wrote to the church at Ephesus, his parting exhortation to them was to be strong in the Lord and in the power of His might (see Eph. 6:10). Not only that, he exhorted them to put on the whole armor of God in order to stand against the wiles of the devil (see Eph. 6:11). His final exhortation to the Ephesians was that they should pray with all kinds of prayer and supplication being watchful to that end (see Eph. 6:18).

On another occasion, writing to the church at Corinth, Paul, referring to Ephesus, spoke of a great and effectual door being opened to advance the Kingdom in Ephesus but nevertheless there were many adversaries.

LESSONS FROM PAUL

So what do we learn from Paul's missionary efforts at Ephesus? Many lessons indeed! First, we see that the disciples were the critical factors behind the impact of the gospel in Ephesus. They ensured that all of Asia heard the gospel. How did this happen? Paul took 12 disciples to the Jewish synagogue; and when they were rejected at the synagogue, he proceeded to the School of Tyranus where they were trained for two and a half years. What did this training involve and why did it take that long?

For a start, we have nothing to tell us what type of church the church at Ephesus was in terms of leadership structure and membership. Regardless, the church had an impact reaching all over Asia.

Most importantly though, we see from Paul's concluding exhortation to the disciples that underlying all they were doing in Ephesus, they were to continue in prayer.

> *Finally, my brethren, be* **strong in the Lord and in the power of His might. Put on the whole armor of God,** *that you may be able to stand against the wiles of the devil. For we do not wrestle against flesh and blood, but against principalities, against powers, against the rulers of the darkness of this age, against spiritual hosts of wickedness in the heavenly places. Therefore take up the whole armor of God, that you may be able to withstand in the evil day, and having done all, to stand. Stand therefore, having girded your waist with truth, having put on the breastplate of righteousness, and having shod your feet with the preparation of the gospel of peace; above all, taking the shield of faith with which you will be able to quench all the fiery darts of the wicked one. And take the helmet of salvation, and the sword of the Spirit, which is the word of God;* **praying always with all prayer and supplication** *in the Spirit, being watchful to this end with all perseverance and supplication for all the saints—and for me, that utterance may be given to me, that I may open my mouth boldly to make known the mystery of the gospel, for which I am ambassador in chains; that in it I may speak boldly, as I ought to speak* (Ephesians 6:10-20).

Paul's parting exhortation was to pray with all kinds of prayer and supplication. The Amplified bible puts it this way:

> *Pray at all times (on every occasion in every season) in the Spirit, with all [manner of] prayer and entreaty. To that end keep alert and watch with strong purpose and perseverance, interceding in behalf of all the saints (God's consecrated people) (Ephesians 6:18).*

The power of prayer in every circumstance cannot be overemphasized. It permeates everything and touches every aspect of human existence. It underlies every kind of endeavor and is the secret behind every kind of success. Every church can find inspiration from the church at Ephesus to influence and transform their community, city, and even nation. All of Asia heard of the exploits of Paul and the 12 disciples.

Unfortunately, many leaders are to quick to copy one gimmick or the other as the means of building their church. When this happens, sooner than later the church becomes introverted in its understanding of its mission. However, when influence and transformation are the driving force behind our aspirations and motivation, our focus is first to train and impart, no matter how few in number. We recognize that success depends first on the quality of impartation we have made and not on the quantity of the people we seek to gather.

So what do we learn about the church at Ephesus? Discipleship must become the fundamental objective of every church. Jesus' parting words in Matthew 28 are "go and make disciples of all nations." When we take time like Paul did with 12 disciples over a two and a half year period, what we will undoubtedly achieve is a group of men and women who are trained and equipped to influence all dimensions of life in a city in the same way that the disciples at Ephesus did. The strength of the church to fulfill the great commission rests on understanding the critical role of discipleship.

My hope is that as leaders and pastors involved in discipleship in one form or another we would be challenged to redesign our church activities to make discipleship central to all that we do. Too many of us are caught up with the never-ending activities of church programs, conferences, meetings, fundraising events, and church planting efforts that we unwittingly reprioritize discipleship to the disadvantage of the men and women God wants to equip to infiltrate cities and transform nations. We must never forget that our first assignment is to disciple men and women.

CHAPTER 11

Prayer and Fasting

*Is this not the **fast** that I have chosen: to loose the bonds of wickedness, to undo the heavy burdens, to let the oppressed go free, and that you break every yoke? Is it not to share your bread with the hungry, and that you bring to your house the poor who are cast out; when you see the naked, that you cover him, and not hide yourself from your own flesh? Then your light shall break forth like the morning, your healing shall spring forth speedily, and your righteousness shall go before you; the glory of the Lord shall be your rear guard (Isaiah 58:6-8).*

*But in all things we commend ourselves as ministers of God: in much patience, in tribulations, in needs, in distresses, in stripes, in imprisonments, in tumults, in labors, in sleeplessness, in **fastings** (2 Corinthians 6:4-5).*

*In weariness and toil, in sleeplessness often, in hunger and thirst, in **fastings** often, in cold and nakedness (2 Corinthians 11:27).*

Fasting is one of the greatest joys anyone can experience. This may sound paradoxical because fasting involves denying your body of food. But it is a joy nevertheless because it is one tool God ordained to allow us to soar in the spirit as eagles. Many times our inner man is caged by our emotions, or our intellect. At other times it is laziness, physical disposition, or infirmity. However when we fast, divine life is infused into our inner man. Fasting weakens our body but it strengthens our spirits.

Humankind is a trinity too—we are made up of spirit, soul, and body. Our spirit is the seat of the re-created life of God that died through sin, but comes alive again after we are reconciled to God through Jesus Christ. Our soul is the center of our intellect, emotions, and will. When God said let us make man in Our image and likeness, our likeness with God was never intended to be physical because God is a Spirit and they who worship God, worship Him in Spirit and in truth. Our likeness to God is a spiritual likeness and not a physical likeness. This is the only way in which billions of sons and daughters of God would look like God irrespective of race, size, etc. So when we fast, the strengthening and rejuvenation of our spirits make us more like God.

As I said earlier, life can seem paradoxical. We live on earth, yet we live by the principles of an unseen realm (the Kingdom of God), worshiping an unseen God who sent His Son to earth in our likeness and had to die to set us free from the sin of rebellion that separated us from God and held us bound in a nature and lifestyle of sin and the flesh under the rule of the devil. What a paradox. Therefore when Jesus came to earth, He came as the life-giving Spirit.

> … There is a natural body, and there is a spiritual body. And so it is written, "The first man Adam became a living being." The last Adam became a **life-giving spirit**. However, the spiritual is not first, but the natural, and afterward the spiritual. The first man was of the earth, made of dust; the second Man is the Lord from heaven. As was the man of dust, so also are those who are made of dust; and as is the heavenly Man, so also are those who are heavenly (1 Corinthians 15:44-48).

Jesus restores us or better still salvages us from an earthbound life and transports us to one that is heavenly because He is the life-giving Spirit. Note the words *"life-giving spirit."* The difference between Jesus our redeemer and Adam our forefather is that while Adam was a living *soul*, Jesus is a life-giving *spirit*. Not only does Jesus give life, He gives life because He is a Spirit. Therefore all who are one family with Jesus, of which He is the Head, must do everything to enhance, nurture, and strengthen the life He imparts to us.

FASTING INFUSES DIVINE LIFE

Fasting is, therefore, one of the means of infusing divine life into our inner selves. When this happens, we are drawn more and more into the real essence of who we are fundamentally—men and women seated in heavenly places far above principalities and powers. While for every believer this position in Heaven is our right, in reality many of us don't experience it because we haven't experienced the joys of fasting. Too many believers allow their inner selves to become famished and malnourished because we are too concerned about food. So we may look well-fed on the outside, but yet our inner selves are emaciated and suffering from long-term malnourishment. Imagine how different life would be if we recognized that essentially we can live on earth, yet carry the ambience, atmosphere, power, compassion, wisdom, and the life of Heaven on a daily basis because we fast often.

One of the reasons Paul had as much revelation and insight as he did was because he fasted often. In the midst of all the challenges Paul faced, fasting still had a significant place in his life. Twice in his letter to the Corinthians, Paul mentions fasting as a regular feature of his lifestyle. The first time he wrote what he described as his commendation as ministers of God to the Corinthian believers, Paul was effectively saying that in the midst of tribulations, needs, distresses, stripes, imprisonment, tumults, labors, and sleeplessness, fasting played a prominent role. Why would Paul describe fasting as one of the points of commendation? It was because he wanted the Corinthians to know some of the secrets of his strength during all he had to go through. Fasting ensured that, though Paul went through great challenges, he nevertheless was strengthened where it mattered most—in the spirit! Paul insulated himself from the challenging circumstances by ensuring that fasting stayed with him regardless of his trials and tribulations.

No matter what we may go through in this life, our greatest source of strength is in the spirit! When we nourish our inner selves by denying our flesh, we ensure that we have the power, life, joy, wisdom, and compassion of God to do the impossible.

The second reason we fast is because fasting is another way to create a supernatural platform for us to be phenomenally successful in whatever God calls us to do. It ensures we function in the power of God. When Jesus reached the age of 30 years, just before He started His public ministry, He was compelled by the Holy Spirit to go into the wilderness and embark on a 40-day fast. When Jesus was led into the wilderness, He was already full of the Holy Spirit (see Luke 4:1). However when He returned after 40 days, He returned in the power of the Holy Spirit (see Luke 4:14). This is the assurance of anyone who wants to live on earth in the power of God.

FASTING RELEASES POWER

Under the guidance of the Holy Spirit, fasting releases power to do whatever we have to do. It cuts across everything. Too many limit the power of God because we don't see that God's power applies to everything. Many marriages can be healed by the power God, released through fasting to walk in respect for each other. Many rebellious teenagers can be led aright—not through beatings and manipulation, but by the power of fasting to show love and restraint to them. In every sphere of life we are to walk in power.

Too many people in our families, offices, and communities never get to know God because we don't do anything practical to reveal God to others through the power that comes through fasting. Imagine how many people can come to salvation not in a church meeting but in our homes, in offices, and in different social settings because of the power we release through fasting. Jesus, though full of the Holy Spirit, didn't take it for granted that He was Jesus the only begotten of the Father. When He preached, those who heard Him said they had never heard anyone speak with such authority. They compared His preaching with the preaching of the scribes and concluded that He preached with authority. This authority was evident because Jesus prayed and fasted.

Fasting should be part of our lifestyle. When Jesus spoke to the disciples, He said to them, when you fast, do not disfigure yourself like the Pharisees do who seek public adulation (see Matt. 6:16). Though we are required to fast often, we do so and carry on as normal. So we ensure we look good so that those around us may not even be aware that we are fasting. When we make it our lifestyle, we allow the power of God to flow through us. We present ourselves as willing vessels to be used by God to change our world.

Today, fasting is seen by some believers as a fast-track method of getting God to answer our prayer. But we must not forget that fasting does not guarantee "our answer." When Isaiah described fasting as a means of loosening the bonds of wickedness, undoing the heavy burdens, letting the oppressed go free, and breaking every yoke, he was making a call to fast to those who would help others (see Isa. 58:6). Unfortunately, our focus has become self-centered. We have changed the focus to ourselves forgetting that if we are in Christ, we are new creations, old things are passed away, behold all things have become new (see 2 Cor. 5:17). Every believer is a new creation. This is a fact! We have to accept it by faith. We must not try to rationalize it based on who we were before salvation came our way or what we had done previously. No matter how terrible we may have been, in Christ old things are passed away. If God says so, then it is a fact. If God says old things have passed away, we must accept it as such. Newness every day is the portion of the believer.

FOCUS ON GOD

...whatever things are true, whatever things are noble, whatever things are just, whatever things are pure, whatever things are lovely, whatever things are of good report, if there is any virtue and if there is anything praiseworthy—meditate on these things (Philippians 4:8).

As long as we meditate on the great things God has done in our lives, we will experience the joy, peace, and life of newness. The problem is we meditate on the past rather than meditating on the present and the future. When our focus is the wonderful works of God in salvation, we become agents for the power of God to loosen the bonds of wickedness that hold many bound in all kinds of sinful practice. This is the correction that Isaiah sought to establish by pointing to the kind of fast that God ordains. Isaiah said our fasting should not be one that is full of strife and contention but rather one in which God can use us to set the oppressed free.

Jesus said:

The Spirit of the Lord is upon Me, because He has anointed Me to preach the gospel to the poor; He has sent Me to heal the brokenhearted, to proclaim liberty to the captives and recovery of sight to the blind, to set at liberty those who are oppressed; to proclaim the acceptable year of the Lord (Luke 4:18-19).

Jesus knew that fasting would break the powers of darkness holding many blind and in captivity. So when we fast, the power that comes to us breaks through spiritual blindness and demonic oppression to pierce the hearts of those we minister to with the everlasting power and love of God. This is the joy of fasting. This is why Jesus, even though He was full of the Holy Spirit, went away to fast for 40 days. He knew He needed the special power of God.

Fasting also helps us live effectively on earth. Our lives on earth require that we experience the reality of being seated in heavenly places far above principalities and powers. Living on earth means that it is easy to be separated from the life, joy, peace, compassion, strength, wisdom, grace, love, self-control, and power that surrounds everyone who sits in heavenly places. Fasting helps anchor us to the supernatural dimension that should accompany our lives daily. Otherwise, we will be limited in dealing with the onslaught of the enemy that assails us on many fronts. Temptations, fears, intimidation, insecurities, and lack of faith are the daily challenges all believers face.

When we fast, we rise above these challenges. When we fast, we are spirit-controlled and can respond appropriately. When we fast, we are less likely to find ourselves doing what we shouldn't be doing. Young couples in courtship should be radical—in addition to all the romantic dinners and outings, they need learn how to fast together. Fasting deals with the temptation of falling into fornication or dangerous sensuality or lewdness in their relationship. It helps maintain the bounds of decency until marriage.

BOLD AND IN CONTROL

Fasting also helps us operate in higher dimensions of faith. When we fast, we are more sensitive and better at discerning what steps to take. We are bolder because we sense the leading and assurance of God to do what God requires of us. Our spirits take control and override the undue caution that our intellect may want to bring to a matter. This is not to say that we should disregard our intellect but to draw attention to the fact that our intellect can stand in the way of God. Intellect is a great blessing from God to help us rule in this life; but in the protocol of the King-dom, the inner man is the seat of government where our fellowship and interaction with the Holy Spirit takes place. Our intellect becomes the platform for executing the will of God after we receive revelation, insight, and direction from God in our spirits.

Many times I embark upon a fast to help me move more purpose-fully and faster in newer dimensions of faith. This helps me stay on the pathway God has ordained, but not just to stay in the pathway but to also thrive in the pathway and bring acceleration and tenacity to my journey. Recently when I sold my equity as a partner in a law firm, many people around me thought I had made a wrong move, even those who should know better. Their attitude taught me a useful lesson. Even those around you, no matter how spiritual they may be, can get used to seeing you operate in your comfort zone. When change comes, they may not discern that it is a season of change. If you don't have faith, you may be unwilling to take a risk, especially if you place an undue premium on the spirituality of others whose affirmation you seek. However, along with a fast, especially a prolonged fast, comes faith to do what is necessary.

Now I must add that fasting by itself will be of little benefit. *Fasting must be accompanied with prayer, Bible study, and meditation.* When we can also get away from the hustle and bustle and the demands of everyday life, the benefits of fasting are even greater. In addition, it is wise to seek medical advice if you have never fasted, or if you are on medication to ensure you do not injure your health.

The Bible records different kinds of fasts. In the Book of Daniel 10:2-3 it is recorded:

> *In those days I, Daniel, was mourning three full weeks. I ate no pleasant food, no meat or wine came into my mouth, nor did I anoint myself at all, till three weeks were fulfilled.*

The Message Bible version states that Daniel "ate only plain and simple food, no seasoning or meat or wine." On the other hand, when Jesus fasted, it was for 40 days without food.

It is, therefore, vitally important for you to find out what works best for you if you decide to fast. Sometimes when I fast, I may not eat regular meals and eat only lightly, having a salad once a day. At other times I may not eat food for three days, but I do drink liquids every so often. Sometimes I fast by skipping a meal. It is important to find your personal rhythm. Please be aware of your body messages. Once I was fasting and taking multivitamins. One morning I woke up feeling faint and went to see a doctor. After asking a few questions, he simply ordered a meal for me and advised me not to take food supplements while fasting.

The important thing is to remember that fasting is denying our bodies food for a season. How we do it and how often must be determined by each of us as we are led by the Spirit of God.

Before fasting for the first time, seriously consider these questions:

1. Should I consult my doctor to make sure my body is healthy enough to fast?

2. Have I asked the Holy Spirit for guidance about fasting?

3. What types of fasting are there?

4. To what kind of fasting should I commit?

5. How often should I fast?

6. How long should I fast?

7. Should I speak to my pastor about fasting?

Listen for God's answers to these questions as you think about including fasting as part of your prayer life.

CHAPTER 12

Taking Responsibility

THE NEHEMIAH PRINCIPLE

Nehemiah, whose name means Yahweh's comfort or comfort of Yahweh, provides us a perfect picture of the partnership between prayer and the burden for transforming nations especially where the spiritual and material conditions are desolate. The first important lesson from the life of Nehemiah is in the power of his name, which finds powerful expression in Nehemiah's role in rebuilding the walls of Jerusalem.

Prior to this time, Israel had been captive due to sin and rebellion against God. Nehemiah too was captive but a favored captive in the court of Artaxerxes, king of Persia, as his cupbearer. When Nehemiah receives news of the conditions of those who remained in the land when the best were carted off as slaves, he weeps and mourns for many days. He wept and mourned because he could feel the pain of God at the desolation of God's heritage. Could it ever be forgotten that Israel was intended as God's special treasure above all people so long as they adhered to the terms of the covenant God had made with them?

So here was a report cataloging the woe that had become the lot of the people of Judah. The people were living in "great distress and reproach." The walls of Jerusalem were broken down and its gates burnt with fire (see Neh. 1:3). These were the conditions that grieved the heart of God and caused His servant Nehemiah, God's comfort, to weep and mourn. Just as in the days of Nehemiah, there are some men and women rising across the nations of the earth who mourn and weep about the desolation of their nations and especially in the midst of national desolation, the desolation of the church of the living God itself.

Like Nehemiah, many are mourning and weeping as they identify with the heart of God who sees His "special treasure" made desolate through sin and rebellion to God's holy ways. God's heart is heavy when He sees men and women bearing His name living in distress and reproach with the walls of the churches broken down as every manner of idolatry finds expression among the leaders of God's people and the people themselves.

GOD'S HEART

In these circumstances, what God seeks first are those who will give Him comfort; men and women who will identify with the pain in God's heart and provide succor. Nehemiah represents a certain kind of leader God is seeking today. These are simply people who desire to comfort God. They will be found in trusted positions where God has placed them for an appointed time. What distinguishes them from everybody else is while others are selfish and self-centered with their influential positions, those who will bring God comfort see their positions of influence as a platform for bringing comfort to God's heart.

I pray as you read this that God will give you a burden to bring comfort to His heart concerning His Church and His nations within your sphere of influence. When believers seek to comfort God, a position of influence doesn't excite them; rather it places a burden in their hearts because they must seek to use that position to bring comfort to God's heart. This is what Nehemiah did. He prayed:

O Lord, I pray, please let Your ear be attentive to the prayer of Your servant, and to the prayer of Your servants who desire to fear Your name; and let Your servant prosper this day, I pray, and grant him mercy in the sight of this man" For I was the king's cupbearer (Nehemiah 1:11).

As the king's cupbearer, Nehemiah was very influential. The king's life rested in his hands. He had to ensure that the king was not poisoned. Yet despite this level of influence, Nehemiah prayed not for himself but for an opportunity to make a difference in the lives of those distressed and discouraged by the conditions in Jerusalem.

And it came to pass in the month of Nisan, in the twentieth year of king Artaxerxes, when wine was before him, that I took the wine and gave it to the king. Now I had never been sad in his presence before. Therefore the king said to me, "Why is your face sad, since you are not sick? This is nothing but sorrow of heart." So I became dreadfully afraid, and said to the king, "May the king live forever! Why should my face not be sad, when the city the place of my fathers' tombs, lies waste, and its gates are burned with fire?" (Nehemiah 2:1-3)

This was a dramatic and swift response to Nehemiah's prayer. He was presented with an opportunity that would enable him to make a difference. It is clear why God wanted Nehemiah to have an opportunity to make a difference. Nehemiah exhibited a level of empathy concerning what mattered to God such that it was inevitable God would make a way for Nehemiah.

FROM BURDEN TO SPIRITUAL ENERGY

The second principle we can glean from Nehemiah is that his deep concern for the conditions he met led to praying and fasting. It is one thing to weep and mourn over the conditions of the church and the state of the nation, but if we leave it at that, then we may end up in depression. In a depressive condition, we cannot bring about any kind of change. This kind of condition only leads to heaviness of soul and discouragement. It may even leave a person vulnerable to demonic attacks. The first response to distress, reproach, and desolation is to turn to God with prayer and fasting.

Nehemiah converted his burden to spiritual energy and life. Remember, weeping may endure for a night (see Ps. 30:5). The point is, after the weeping we must respond to God with an acceptable sacrifice. As Hosea says:

> *Come and let us return to the Lord; for He has torn, but He will heal us; He has stricken, but He will bind us up. After two days He will revive us; on the third day He will raise us up, that we may live in His sight* (Hosea 6:1-2).

Every burden bearer must first return to the Lord. We must return with the confidence that though we have been torn, Jehovah will heal. If He finds a burden bearer, God will heal and bind up the wounds of His distressed and reproached people.

Nehemiah's first task in prayer is to take responsibility for the sins of the people. National transformation, or for that matter church transformation, cannot come about until the root causes of desolation are properly addressed. The root cause for the desolation Israel suffered was sin and separation from the ways of God. It was this primary problem that Nehemiah first sought to address before God.

> *I pray, Lord God of heaven, O great and awesome God, You who keep Your covenant and mercy with those who love You and observe Your commandments, please let Your ear be attentive and Your eyes open, that You may hear the prayer of Your servant which I pray before You now, day and night for the children of Israel which we have sinned against You. Both my father's house and I have sinned. We have acted very corruptly against You, and have not kept the commandments,*

the statutes, nor the ordinances which You commanded Your servant Moses (Nehemiah 1:5-7).

Every burden bearer must identify with the sins of the people as not just their sin, but as something for which there is collective guilt before God.

When we identify with the sin of the land or the people of whom we are part, what that does is release brokenness before God. It shows that our view of sin and unrighteousness transcends what we may have done personally. We identify with the broken nature of men and women and society and its institutions the way God would. This is actually what Jesus did. When He hung on the cross, He identified with the sin for which He had no part. A Man completely without sin, but for the sake of you and me was laden with the sin of the world. This single act broke the back of principalities and powers because the power of sin is death—and Jesus faced death, conquered it, and became the template for the new kind of post-sin existence called resurrected life.

TRANSFORMATION

In the same way, when we identify with the collective sin of the people or the nation, we break the power of principalities and powers because we say to God we repent not just for what we have done but also for what we all have done. Anyone who takes that position symbolically reenacts what Jesus did. As many sin and their sin defiles the people and the nation, so the repentance of one for all has the power to begin the process of transformation in a nation.

When this happens, God opens a great door of opportunity for remedial action. God orchestrated circumstances that allowed Nehemiah to visit Jerusalem and begin the process of change and transformation. Nehemiah went before the king and Nehemiah's sad countenance, which itself was unacceptable, opens up an opportunity for the king of Persia to be the instrument through whom Nehemiah would be sent to Jerusalem. Thereafter Nehemiah visits Jerusalem, views the conditions of desolation and rallies the nobles to rise up to the task of rebuilding the ruined city (see Neh. 3).

Everything that happened thereafter was the result of taking one oar of the burden for Jerusalem and adding a second oar of prayer to navigate the boat of destiny such that the people all rose up to rebuild. Nehemiah reveals principles of national transformation. First a burden, then prayer, and then the strategies for rallying the nobles to arise and collectively make a difference. Around the world God desires to anoint burden bearers afresh—men and women who will carry the burden to see nationwide transformation and who are willing to pay the price in prayer and thereafter roll up their sleeves and put the bricks one atop the other in the rebuilding process.

Many who pray don't like getting their hands dirty in the business of national transformation. They feel that after prayer God should all by Himself bring about the desired change. Nehemiah defies this attitude. After prayer was done, he went to Jerusalem, surveys the broken down conditions, and leads the nobles to rebuild.

Each one of us must take time to identify the broken communities in which we live. As we do, God's heart of compassion will break forth triggering a continuous flow of divine strength and life to identify problems, pray, and then resolve the issues that need to be resolved. This applies to the local church as well.

THE LOCAL CHURCH AND PRAYER

"Even them I will bring to My holy mountain, and make them joyful in My house of prayer. Their burnt offerings and their sacrifices will be accepted on My altar; for My house shall be called a house of prayer for all nations." The Lord God, who gathers the outcasts of Israel, says, "Yet I will gather to him others besides those who are gathered to him" (Isaiah 56:7-9).

To the intent that now the manifold wisdom of God might be made known by the church to the principalities and powers in the heavenly places (Ephesians 3:10).

Establishing a corporate prayer ministry brings a dimension of spiritual strength, order, vibrancy, and government to a local assembly. The primary tool for establishing God's authority, power, life, and purpose in a local assembly is through prayer. The strength of a local assembly can easily be discerned from its culture of prayer. The influence and impact of the people in a local assembly can be measured by the life and vibrancy of prayer as an integral part of the life of its people. The first task of every church is to establish prayer as the heartbeat of the church.

George Barna, in his book *The Habits of Highly Effective Churches*, says there are six pillars of effective churches: worship, evangelism, Christian education, community among the believers, stewardship, and serving the needy. I would add prayer. From experience, while George Barna is right, I have found that one additional ingredient—if not the central ingredient—is *prayer*.

TRAIN AND EQUIP

Every local assembly is called to train and equip believers who will express the image of Christ and ultimately the Kingdom of God through their lives and through their ministry on earth. When this happens, the church can be said to express governing capacity. When the nature of Christ is evident in the people and the people are pursuing purpose and spreading the influence of God's Kingdom in transforming people and institutions, the church evidently can be said to be a governing territorial church. In other words, the church is relevant and effective as the salt of the earth and the light of the world. This is one of the foundational reasons for a prayer ministry. Every pastor who wants to see strong, well-equipped believers fully expressing the kingly and priestly dimensions of the call of God will, of necessity, pay serious attention to recruiting and grooming men and women to create an atmosphere of spiritual government in their local assembly. This is actually the best model of church to establish in order to fulfill the great commission of discipling nations.

> Ask of Me the nations for your inheritance and the uttermost
> parts of the earth for your possession (Psalm 2:8).

The primary mandate of every church is to take over the spiritual atmosphere in the nations where it is located. Depending on how visionary and daring the leaders of local churches want to be, this sphere of influence can cut across the boundaries of multiple nations. So we can take a nation or nations as our inheritance. This occurs first in the spiritual then later in the natural. This is vital to the role of the church in any locality. Consistently throughout the New Testament we see the connection between the spread of the gospel of the Kingdom and influence over nations. When Paul trained 12 men in Ephesus, the Bible later records that all of Asia heard the gospel. The first assignment of every church is to take control of the spiritual atmosphere.

Churches that carry a burden for the nations and see the nations of the earth as geographic areas over which God's spiritual laws must rule must seek to establish prayer ministries that train and equip believers with the experience of power with God in prayer.

Prayer Ministry

On a practical note, another reason for establishing a prayer ministry in a local church is because it provides unparalleled training for anyone seeking to learn to pray anyway. Too many churches discover that their members lack understanding about the diverse and rich nature of prayer. Too often some have one revelation of prayer and camp around that revelation to the detriment of growth and maturity in a wholesome manner. Corporate fellowship and prayer provide a healthy environment for many to become disciples and to grow in the knowledge of Jesus Christ. Prayer is also an engine room providing the spiritual force to break demonic conspiracies that the devil orchestrates to hamper the advance of God's Kingdom.

As mentioned previously in Chapter 1, the church offered constant prayer for Peter after King Herod killed James:

> *Now about that time Herod the King stretched out his hand to harass some from the church. Then he killed James the brother of John with the sword. And because he saw that it pleased the Jews, he proceeded further to seize Peter also. Now it was during the Days of Unleavened Bread. So when he had arrested him, he put him in prison, and delivered him to four squads of soldiers to keep him, intending to bring him before the people after Passover. So Peter was therefore kept in prison, but constant prayer was offered to God for him by the church (Acts 12:1-5).*

This Scripture provides an excellent illustration of the power of a praying community of believers. Herod had just beheaded James. When Herod observed that the beheading of James pleased the Jews, he arrested Peter. Now if the church had been slow to react with the arrest of James, they needed no prompting regarding what to do when Peter was arrested. The imminence of another beheading galvanized them to pray. They gathered together and began to pray. This was not a matter for which they had to petition Herod. Doing so would have been a grave misunderstanding of the issues at stake. So the disciples who gathered to pray offered unceasing prayer to God for Peter to be released.

Their prayer led to dramatic results. An angel went into the jail and appeared beside Peter who was sleeping bound with two chains between two soldiers with guards also guarding the prison door. Then, dramatically, as the angel woke up Peter, he stood up and the chains fell off Peter. The angel then led Peter out of the prison before disappearing when they came out unto the street. These unprecedented events came about because the church rose up in one accord to pray. God ordains power with the potential for dramatic results when the church prays.

In every city of the world, churches have the opportunity to see the dramatic dimension of God's power when they come together to pray. The events were so dramatic that when Peter arrived at the door of the home where the disciples were gathered praying, none believed it really was Peter at the door.

Every local assembly must expect to deal with all kinds of demonic opposition, too. It may not be imprisonment as in Peter's case, but it will be opposition nevertheless. As a pastor, I have experienced firsthand the opposition of the devil to our mission as a church. In many instances when we seek to have some permanence in a location with land acquisition, we have faced tremendous opposition from landowners to bureaucratic delays in getting regulatory approvals. At other times, we have had to contend with ill health, strife, and discouragement. But as we stood firm in prayer, we saw the miraculous breakthrough of God.

Direct Spiritual Benefits

To establish a prayer ministry requires appealing to a mix of people. This involves identifying those who already have an experience of intercession and enjoy praying. It also involves recruiting people who want to learn to pray. It can be one of the most exciting assignments to undertake. It can also be very tough. It can be exciting because it is one ministry in which what you do has a direct spiritual benefit on all those involved. Many ministries in a local assembly in themselves do not provide a direct spiritual benefit; so, for instance, if I am in a counseling team, I find that many times after counseling I am emotionally and physically drained. The reason for this is not far-fetched. It is because I have been involved in dealing with all kinds of emotional issues and challenging circumstances.

However, when I gather with others to intercede, even though my prayer is focused on the needs of others, the fact that I am praying has a beneficial impact on me as well. So people who join a prayer ministry find that they generally become better for it. They become more spiritual in their disposition and outlook to life. They hear God better. They become more compassionate and show more fruit of the Spirit. In addition, many who start out in the prayer ministry go on to lead in other capacities because of the grace and strength they receive. It can also be exciting because of the opportunity to see people exercising the different gifts of the Holy Spirit.

When motivating people to join the prayer ministry, these facts must be made very clear. People must not think they are coming to join a group of superspiritual people to pray. They must see that it is a privilege, which has the added benefit of personal transformation on a monumental scale.

Having said that, getting people committed to praying can be very tough too. Prayer is not seen as a glamorous or enjoyable activity especially when it is realized that commitment is vital. Therefore anyone who heads a prayer ministry must have strong pastoral, teaching, and intercessory gifts. As it may be difficult to have all these gifts present in one person at any one time or when it is required, what works is a partnership with the senior pastor and someone with strong intercessory and/or teaching grace heading the ministry. The pastor brings clear visionary direction to the prayer ministry. The pastor infuses the ministry with a clear sense of the mandate of the church and the role of the prayer ministry to watch over those in the prayer. This energizes everyone in prayer because they see the direct connection between prayer and the advancement of the mission of the church.

Motivation to pray is enhanced and the ownership of the vision is shared crucially among people who are willing to do what needs to be done to see the vision fulfilled. In addition, the pastor can bring a nurturing and mentoring grace to those who join the prayer ministry. When this happens, the people are strengthened and discover the joys of walking with Jesus. This in turn motivates others to join the prayer ministry as they observe the transformative power of service in the local assembly.

Partnerships

Ideally the pastor should work in partnership with a functioning head with strong intercessory gifts. This allows the pastor to still exercise oversight but not be burdened with the daily activity of prayer. With a functional head in the person of someone with passion to pray and a strong intercessory disposition, everyone in the prayer ministry can experience depth, power, and the activation of spiritual gifts. The prayer ministry becomes a place for the manifestation of strength. In such an atmosphere, many more leaders are groomed who may play roles in the prayer ministry or find expression in other areas of ministry. I have found from practical experience that the bulk of dynamic leaders who take on pastoral responsibilities or go on to lead as strong heads of other ministries have been those groomed in the prayer ministry.

This partnership between pastoral oversight and intercessory passion allows for the synergy of the grace for intercession and leadership oversight. It also allows the functional intercessor head of ministry time to grow and discover other dimensions of ministry which may be dormant, waiting for the appointed time for expression.

With this partnership in place, the prayer ministry can grow in leaps and bounds—people are groomed in an atmosphere of nurture, fellowship, discipleship, and service. Passion and zeal for the vision of the local assembly grows and spreads. As a result, the passion for prayer spreads within the larger, corporate church.

Administration

The next key element in running an effective prayer ministry is administration. A database of membership has to be managed effectively, especially when the people involved exceed a certain number. For instance, once a ministry is in the region of 30 members and above, a proper administrative structure is required. So for people to pray regularly, hold prayer vigils, conduct retreats, and carry prayer burdens, they will require regular fellowship, motivation, revelatory teaching, and pastoral oversight. This process requires proper administrative oversight.

On a practical note, many find that as soon as they increase their commitment to pray, they also face increased pressures from the devil to test their resolve to stay committed to prayer. This is natural and to be expected. Everything meaningful—especially prayer—will be resisted by the devil. It is important, therefore, to have regular fellowship and a strong feedback mechanism in the prayer ministry. This will encourage and motivate everyone to be steadfast in faith, resisting all the wiles of the devil.

CHAPTER 13

The Gethsemane Principle

Coming out, He went to the Mount of Olives, as He was accustomed and His disciples also followed Him. When He came to the place, He said to them, "Pray that you may not enter into temptation." And He was withdrawn from them about a stone's throw, and He knelt down and prayed, saying, "Father, if it is Your will, take this cup away from Me; nevertheless not My will, but Yours be done." Then an angel appeared to Him from heaven, strengthening Him. And being in agony, He prayed more earnestly. Then His sweat became like great drops of blood falling down to the ground. When He rose up from prayer, and had come to His disciples, He found them sleeping from sorrow. Then He said to them, "Why do you sleep? Rise and pray, lest you enter into temptation" (Luke 22:39-46).

And He came out and went, as was His habit, to the Mount of Olives, and the disciples also followed Him. And when He came to the place, He said to them, Pray that you may not [at all] enter into temptation. And He withdrew from them about a stone's throw and knelt down and prayed. Saying, Father, if You are willing, remove this cup from Me; yet not

My will, but [always] Yours be done. And there appeared to Him an angel from heaven, strengthening Him in spirit. And being in agony [of mind], He prayed [all the] more earnestly and intently, and His sweat became like great clots of blood dropping down upon the ground. And when He got up from prayer, He came to the disciples and found them sleeping from grief, and He said to them, Why do you sleep? Get up and pray that you may not enter [at all] into temptation (Luke 22:39-46 AMP).

The devil our adversary is a deadly foe. He is never weary of battle. He never really gives up. He is always pushing and prodding to find openings he can take advantage of in our battle with him. We can never be lulled into a false sense of security. Even though all may be well and everything is going well, we must never lower our guard. The Bible is full of the examples of godly men and women whose tragic mistakes underline how deadly the enemy is.

All it took was for David to be in the wrong place at the wrong time and see Bathsheba naked; this was the beginning of satan's bait that ultimately culminated in the orchestrated killing of Uriah, Bathsheba's husband. This folly opened the doorway for satan in David's home. Thereafter, even though God had forgiven David's sin, nevertheless Nathan told David that the sword would never depart from his home. David, by his action, opened the door to violence in his family.

Moses one day was fed up with the complaints of the Israelites and so in frustration struck the rock to provide water for the Israelites rather than speak to the rock as God had directed. This single act of disobedience cost Moses dearly. He never made it to the Promised Land, much as he pleaded with God.

Uzziah was a king who started out very well. He became king as a teenager at the age of 16 years. Zechariah the prophet who had understanding in the visions of God was available and so Uzziah sought God in the days of Zechariah. And God made him prosper on every side. He defeated the Philistines and the Ammonites and his fame spread all the way to Egypt. But after he had become very strong, Uzziah's heart "was lifted up." In other words, he became proud and forgot the source of his success. He took on a priestly role; he went into the tabernacle and sought to burn incense. This was an act reserved for the priests (the descendants of Aaron). Azariah and 80 other brave priests resisted Uzziah. Rather than retreat in repentance, Uzziah got furious and while the censer used in burning incense was still in his hand, leprosy appeared on his forehead and began to spread. So the priests quickly thrust him out of the tabernacle. In fact, the Bible records that Uzziah himself left the tabernacle hurriedly. For this act of pride, he lost the throne. He had to live in an isolated house for the rest of his life as a leper. What a tragic end to an illustrious life.

I have chosen examples of people who started out well, with a hunger and passion to please God. David, Moses, and Uzziah are heroes of the faith. Their great exploits stand out for all to see and emulate. Their intention was never to disobey God or fall short of the destiny God had ordained. They wanted to end well. They were heroes in their day. The entire nation depended on what direction they gave. The fortunes of many were dependent on what they did.

Imagine the tragedy of knowing that David, who could write so many psalms declaring his love and consecration to God, could orchestrate the murder of a man to cover up his adultery and subsequent marriage. How did the devil blind him to the fact that God is ever-seeing and ever-knowing? How was he blinded to the fact that the devil was setting him up for destruction? This is the tragedy of failing to recognize that the devil is a deadly foe. Every believer must recognize that the devil is locked in mortal combat with us. He never gives up. He never relents. He may leave you for a while, but it is only until another opportune time presents itself.

The Devil's Objective

The primary objective of the devil is to nullify or truncate the destinies and ultimately the influence of every believer on the face of the earth. We must see this side by side with the objective of Jesus on the cross. When Jesus died, it was ultimately to ensure that a new breed of men and women would multiply on the earth—looking like Jesus, talking like Jesus, feeling like Jesus, thinking like Jesus, and like Jesus going about anointed with the Holy Spirit and with power doing good, bringing healing to sickness in body, soul, spirit, and institutions everywhere, reconciling all things to our Father and breaking the bondage of futility to which even creation is subject.

Our destiny, therefore, carries the mandate of obliterating the works of darkness in any form. So the minute anyone is focused on spreading the fragrance, the power, the life, and the very essence of Christ into any facet of human interaction, they come up against a battle. The prince of this world, satan, will fight and do all he can to neutralize such a person.

Another good illustration of this deadly battle with the devil is Daniel's experience. First satan attempted to compromise Daniel with the king's delicacies, which would have defiled Daniel because this was against the Jewish law. When Daniel refused to be defiled, satan raised the level of opposition by orchestrating genocide against all the wise men in the land for refusing not just to interpret Nebuchadnezzar's dream but worse still for not knowing what the dream was in the first place! To the undiscerning this was a battle in which Daniel was a not the central target. However, to the discerning observer, Daniel was the chief target. The devil was subtle and so the attack was not direct.

Daniel took the initiative and went to the king's chief executioner, Arioch, to ask for time while he and his Hebrew friends went to God in prayer. God heard the cry of Daniel and his friends and revealed the dream and its interpretation. After proclaiming that Daniel's God was the only true God for revealing the dream and its interpretation, this same Nebuchadnezzar would erect a golden image for all to bow down to and worship and put Daniel's friends in the fiery furnace for refusing to bow down and worship the golden image. Daniel would later end up in the lion's den because the enemy wanted to cut off the spiritual supply line of prayer. This is how vicious and unrelenting the enemy is.

Again when the enemy realized that he could not overcome Daniel with threats of violence and intimidation, he took the battle to another level. He decided to engage the angelic hosts who were on their way to give Daniel understanding concerning his role as a prophet. So the angel Gabriel said to Daniel that from the day Daniel started seeking God and fasting 21 days, the angel was dispatched to bring understanding; but the prince of Persia withstood him 21 days. In other words, for each day Daniel fasted, the demonic hosts withstood the angel Gabriel (see Dan. 10:12-13).

This illustration from Daniel's experience shows that the enemy's strategy is to fight relentlessly. He doesn't allow himself any rest or thoughts of defeat. Kings have fallen to his relentless power. Families have been destroyed by his relentless onslaught. Businesses have crumbled as they succumbed to his relentless ways. Many pastors, bishops, and church leaders have lost their influence and have seen their destinies destroyed by his relentless power. This is why he never gives up. He succeeds very often and so has every incentive to continue fighting. He knows he has overcome many in the past, and he is therefore emboldened to stay steadfast in his mission.

What is more, he knows that many who succumbed where mighty men and women. Therefore he is encouraged all the more to discover what would make a man or woman succumb to his wiles and attacks. The mightier the better, because the fall of one who is mighty has a greater negative impact; others begin to think *What's the point. Let's eat and be merry for tomorrow we die anyway.*

There Is Always Hope

Is there any hope in these circumstances? Certainly! The best example of hope is Jesus Christ. He provides the most wonderful example of the lifestyle and strategies for overcoming the wiles of the devil. Jesus was born from above and is therefore above all. His lifestyle was superior, His attitude superior, and consecration ever intact. Jesus showed the superiority of the wisdom of God over every ploy of satan. He showed He had access to the superior wisdom of God. He is our best and most potent example. As joint heirs with Christ, we have a right to everything Jesus has. We have access to the wisdom, lifestyle, power, and life that He had on earth. We must never settle for anything less. There is no prayer formula, mantra, or ritual that can match the power of the revelation of who we are and the resources we have in Jesus Christ.

As a young believer, one of the outstanding principles of prayer I learned was the principle of fighting your battles before they manifest. Jesus presents the best template for understanding this dimension of prayer—overcoming the future battles the enemy places in the way as we march toward the fulfillment of every aspect of destiny and purpose. This principle has helped heighten my awareness of destiny from a prophetic perspective and the steps I need to take to overcome the hurdles, the challenges, and the temptations I will of necessity need to overcome on the journey.

As followers of Jesus Christ, we have to constantly remind ourselves that Christianity is a battle. It is a life and death battle and every day there are casualties of war, men and women completely unaware of the seriousness of the battle and what is at stake. These casualties are reflected in many areas of life. Failed marriages, divided families, failed businesses, divided churches, financial compromise, etc.

When Jesus was faced with the greatest battle of His life—going to the cross—we see that His response to this battle provides much to learn from. Dying on the cross was a necessary prelude to Jesus' resurrection in power and life. For Jesus to conquer death, He had to go to the cross. The cross, as painful as it was, could not be avoided. For everyone there are aspects of our destiny that are unavoidable. We cannot wish them away or for that matter pray them away. These unavoidable milestones in the journey of life are part of the tapestry of destiny that God weaves into our future. The sooner we realize this the better for us.

There is a common fallacy about Jesus: because He was the only begotten of the Father, therefore He didn't have the same challenges normal people do. In other words, Jesus could approach the cross differently because in essence He was God. But this is not true. In the garden of Gethsemane, Jesus did ask if the "cup" of destiny could be taken from Him. It was in prayer that He overcame His will and submitted in obedience to the Father's will. He wrestled with the enormity of what He had to do.

We cannot begin to imagine what it must have been like to confront death as a necessary part of the package of destiny. The writer of Hebrews, describing Jesus, said, "though He was a son, He learned obedience by the things which He suffered" (Heb. 5:8).

Journey Milestones

Our first task, therefore, is recognizing the milestones in our journey with the Lord. These milestones may come as tests to show whether we are ready to obey God in all circumstances. I remember years ago I had been the pastor of a branch of a denomination in Scandinavia. After a year, my senior pastor requested that I join him in starting a new church in London during very trying times. It actually led to the temporary rupture of some relationships and ultimately to leaving the denomination. It was a tough time.

I could have stayed on in Scandinavia and avoided the strife and rupture that ensued. But in leaving Scandinavia for London to start this new church, I embraced a new season in my destiny in the midst of it all. My time in Scandinavia was over. I had to hand it over to a Danish citizen. Could I handle the challenge ahead? Only time would tell. To think that my destiny was being unveiled in those circumstances was at the time difficult to fathom. But in truth it was. I learned to hear the voice of God in those circumstances. My one regret was that I wasn't mature enough to handle some of the challenges that came. Nevertheless I learned lifelong lessons that are still relevant to me today.

Jesus had to overcome an exceedingly sorrowful situation. This was the pain He had to overcome. Life doesn't always come in neat packages where everything is just the way we think it should be. God permits different circumstances that help promote the destiny He has ordained. They may come in painful situations, but they are signposts on our journey. Prayer becomes our lifeline in these circumstances—it allows us adequate preparation. It brings a sense of clarity, a sense of resolve and strength to our hearts. At times like these we can succumb to the challenge or the pain that pockmarks our journey. Succumbing to pain and discouragement is what the devil expects us to do.

This was the strategy the devil deployed against Elijah. Fundamentally, I believe Elijah's destiny went beyond executing the 400 prophets of Baal and turning the nation of Israel to repentance. It was a very significant high point, but it was not all that God clearly had in mind. God desired to put other things in place to ensure that what Elijah achieved on Mount Carmel would be the beginning of a new era. So the vicious counter attack that Jezebel started by striking fear in his heart with her threats was aimed at curtailing what had begun. This shows us the deadly and relentless nature of the warfare we are involved in.

So while Jesus went to the Mount of Olives to pray His way through the battles ahead, Elijah went to the wilderness to ask God to take his life. Sorrow and discouragement are deadly tools of the enemy. There was much ahead for Elijah to do and so Jezebel the daughter of the High Priest of Baal released a spirit of intimidation that sought to crush Elijah. However, God had another plan. He fed, strengthened, and refreshed Elijah before sending him on to Horeb, the mountain of God, where he would meet with God and get fresh marching orders. On the mountain of God, Jezebel would fade away in insignificance. I have often wondered why he could only carry one out of the three instructions God gave Him on the mountain.

God had said anoint Hazael king over Syria; also anoint Jehu king over Israel, and Elisha as prophet in your stead. Of these three assignments, only the anointing of Elisha as prophet could be ascribed to Elijah. I have often wondered why, for instance, it took Elisha to send a prophet to anoint Jehu king over Israel. What hindered Elijah from doing this?

Intense Prayer

Jesus' prayer in the garden of Gethsemane is the only prayer recorded in the Bible that describes prayer at the level of intensity Jesus exhibited. Jesus' prayer was so intense that his sweating is described as "great drops of blood falling to the ground." The Amplified Bible describes it as "clots of blood" (Luke 22:44). When dealing with our adversary the devil, there is only one posture he recognizes—the posture of intensity. Elijah's prayer could evoke the mercy of God, but Jesus' prayer overcame the powers of darkness.

So while Elijah went to complain to God about how discouraged he was feeling because of the threats he received from Jezebel, we see a different response from Jesus. Even though Jesus said My soul is exceedingly sorrowful, even unto death He stayed in the place of prayer. He fell on His face before God and prayed earnestly. He did not succumb to the sorrow that sought to overwhelm Him. The devil fears passionate, fervent prayer.

There is something about praying passionately and fervently that overwhelms the devil. We must never forget this fact. Never allow your emotions rule; in the face of the most trying circumstances, fall on your face before God and pray with intensity, fervency, and passion.

Whenever you desire to pray fervently, the enemy will seek to overcome you with sorrow and sleep. Never succumb to it. It is a deception. The human body is far stronger than we imagine. You have infinitely far more capacity than you think. If you feel sorrowful and weary, the first thing to do is pray until the weariness and sorrow have been overcome. You may still feel the weight of what lies ahead, but now it will be supported by the strength and resolve that comes from fervent praying. This was the point Jesus kept making to the disciples who had gone to the garden of Gethsemane with Him. Matthew's account of the events in the garden is very illustrative. Jesus said to them:

> *"My soul is exceedingly sorrowful, even unto death, stay here and watch with Me." He went a little farther and fell on His face, and prayed, saying, "O My Father, if it is possible, let this cup pass from Me; nevertheless, not as I will, but as You will." Then He came to the disciples and found them sleeping, and said to Peter, "What? Could you not watch with Me one hour? Watch and pray, lest you fall into temptation. The spirit indeed is willing, but the flesh is weak"* (Matthew 26:38-41).

However, it is not enough to know that fervent and passionate prayer overwhelm the devil. What is important is to deploy this kind of prayer on every occasion when it is required. Elijah knew about the power of passionate and fervent praying. This is why James wrote:

> *…The effective, fervent prayer of a righteous man avails much. Elijah was a man with a nature like ours, and he prayed earnestly that it would not rain; and it did not rain on the land for three years and six months. And he prayed again, and the heaven gave rain, and the earth produced its fruit* (James 5:16-18).

In other words, Elijah had experienced fervent prayer that resulted in changed circumstances. He had prayed that there would be no rain and God honored his prayer. And then he prayed for rain and God honored his prayer. This kind of fervency must be deployed at all times. It must be evident on every occasion when we confront our eternal adversary. We must never give in to fear, intimidation, sorrow, or discouragement.

The key product of effective and fervent prayer is power. The Amplified Bible describes it like this:

> *…The earnest (heartfelt, continued) prayer of a righteous man makes tremendous power available [dynamic in its working]* (James 5:16).

We must learn from Elijah to never relent when it comes to exhibiting power in the place of prayer. We must resist every temptation to come to God paralyzed by fear, insecurity, or grumbling. You may have experienced the power of effective and fervent prayer in the past. It is not intended to be something we experience occasionally. Our experience must be regular and consistent. This is how we defeat our foe, the devil.

REJOICE IN THE LORD

When the devil recognizes that he cannot compromise our consecration to God, he seeks to truncate our destiny. He seeks to introduce fear into our hearts concerning our readiness to pay the price, and if necessary the ultimate price, in order to fulfill our destiny. When we are confronted with devilish plots on this level, we need to remember that Jesus traveled this route and overcame the devil. What is at stake is the glory of God resting upon mortals. When sin entered the world, what we lost was the glory of God. For all have sinned and fall short of the glory of God (see Rom. 3:23). Sin compromises the glory of God in the life of a man or woman. However, this is just level one of the battle we face with our adversary, the devil.

We must rejoice in the Lord always because He has defeated our foe the devil and gives us the tools for fighting every battle that lies ahead. We are destined to win every time. God has the answer to every situation and provides Jesus our great High Priest as the perfect example of purposeful living and purpose victory.

Ultimately, when Judas Iscariot arrived with the soldiers to arrest Jesus, though he was a traitor, Jesus greeted him with the words, "Friend, why have you come." Jesus could say this because He had already won the victory and was ready for the last lap to the cross. He would face Pilate, Herod, the beatings by Roman soldiers, the scourging, the mockery, and finally the cross and not be deterred. Not once did He lose His cool, complain, or become discouraged. Even when Peter denied Him, Jesus remained resolute and steadfast to the end.

About the Author

Kemela Okara is a lawyer, pastor, author, and politician. He trained as an English barrister and practices law in Nigeria. He was also a missionary with The Redeemed Christian Church of God. Kemela is the resident pastor of This Present House in Lagos, Nigeria. He sits on the board of KSF Micro Finance Bank and is a trustee of Freedom Foundation.

Additional copies of this book and other book titles
from DESTINY IMAGE™ EUROPE
are available at your local bookstore.

We are adding new titles every month!

To view our complete catalog online, visit us at:

www.eurodestinyimage.com

Send a request for a catalog to:

Via della Scafa 29/14
65013 Città Sant'Angelo (Pe) - ITALY
Tel. +39 085 4716623 ◆ +39 085 8670146
info@eurodestinyimage.com

"Changing the world, one book at a time."

Are you an author?
Do you have a "today" God-given message?

CONTACT US

We will be happy to review your manuscript
for the possibility of publication:

publisher@eurodestinyimage.com
http://www.eurodestinyimage.com/pages/AuthorsAppForm.htm